Baton Twirling

(Frontispiece). Surprising as it may seem at first, baton work includes stationary positions, such as the Waist Stationary (left) and the Drum Major's Stationary (right), as well as twirling. During long parades and routines, well-performed stationaries are very smart and snappy and give the twirler a chance to rest tired arms.

BATON TWIRLING

The Fundamentals of an Art
and a Skill

by Constance Atwater

Charles E. Tuttle Company
Rutland · Vermont : Tokyo · Japan

Representatives
For Continental Europe:
BOXERBOOKS, INC., Zurich
For the British Isles:
PRENTICE-HALL INTERNATIONAL, INC., London
For Australasia:
PAUL FLESCH & CO., PTY. LTD., Melbourne

Published by the Charles E. Tuttle Company, Inc.
of Rutland, Vermont & Tokyo, Japan
with editorial offices at
Suido 1-chome, 2–6, Bunkyo-ku, Tokyo

Copyright in Japan, 1964
by Charles E. Tuttle Company, Inc.

Library of Congress Catalog Card No. 64–22749

First printing, 1964

Book design and typography by K. Ogimi
Layout of plates by H. Doki

PRINTED IN JAPAN

Dedicated to all of you
who have a love for and an interest in
the spinning silver shaft

Table of Contents

List of Illustrations

Introduction

THE SILVER shaft spins around and around, glittering in the bright sunlight or sparkling in the glowing footlights. The ease and grace with which the performer exhibits her skill makes you think, "I can do that," and *that* you can, for I shall explain in this book the art and skill of baton twirling.

This is truly an American skill. While other nations boast of their ballet masters, we Americans can boast of our baton masters. In the past ten years, baton twirling has gained such popularity that our foreign neighbors are showing an increasing interest in it. Some of our colleges even offer scholarships to outstanding twirlers, and almost every American school of any size has its colorful marching groups and majorettes.

The history of baton twirling is sketchy, much of it deriving from guess or hearsay, and its actual origin is unknown. The most popular guess is that it is related to the colorful Swiss flag swinging which came to this country along with the Dutch when they settled in Pennsylvania. Another is that it originated at Millsap College in Mississippi. Here, shortly after the Civil War, the well-known Major Millsap founded a college. His "lady athletes" were called the Majorettes, and it is possible that this is the origin of our present-day high-stepping majorettes' name.

However, we do know that the art of baton twirling is relatively new. It was not until early in the 19th century that the conductor's baton was first used as a visual aid to beating time. In 1776, when the first band of any importance, the

United States Marine Band, was organized, the baton was not in use.

We also know that baton twirling seemed to develop on a regional basis, and this accounts for the various differences in terminology. Interested students, teachers, and groups developed individual terms, and you will find, for example, that the terms pitches, aerials, and throws, all mean the same. Improvised twirls are often named by the person who develops them, and, because in twirling improvisation plays a great part, twirls that are similar or even identical often bear different names. You yourself will probably improvise and name twirls before completing this book.

In the early 1930's the drum majorette was unique. Frequently she was the only one of her sex in a parade, stepping high in front of the formation. The high, prancing strut and the spinning baton added much color to civic, military, or school bands. The drum majorette was top banana of the campus, envied by the girls watching from the sidelines, who decided that they, too, would like to be drum majorettes. Thus the popularity and size of the marching groups grew, and baton twirling became an increasingly popular American institution. Marching and twirling have become complicated by the addition of intricate dance steps as well as complex twirling. Mastering the choreography of baton twirling routines now requires highly developed skills, based on training and practice. The results are right out of this world!

This book is designed to help you learn twirling and marching and to organize a performing group, whether you are a member of a school, college, or club, or whether you want to form a private unit and, possibly, later find a sponsor for it. Whichever of these categories you represent, the fundamentals in setting up such a group are the same. The only difference is that once you are organized, trained, and ready to go, the private group has just one more step (if it wishes)—to find a sponsor, about which more later. How to start? Let's turn to Chapter 1.

1

Organizing a Twirling Group

WHILE it is impossible for every baton twirler to become a drum majorette, or to win a scholarship, or to lead the big band, there is fun and excitement for all who participate in marching and baton twirling groups. You will learn that it is easy and rewarding as well to organize your own group.

First, you must publicize your idea, and this may be done in a number of ways. Your sponsor may do it for you. Or you may announce it at your club, your school, or pass the news to your friends. Arrange a time and a place for a meeting and invite anyone who is interested, regardless of previous knowledge of or experience in marching and twirling.

Interest and enthusiasm are the most important requirements. You will find that skill will develop quickly if these two qualities are present. Often novices who practice diligently soon surpass experienced twirlers.

At your first meeting and before any tryouts are held, you must explain clearly what membership will involve. The lesson schedule should be set and the required practice hours established. Lessons may be held in your yard or in a park, if weather and climate permit, or in a school auditorium or gym. Sometimes a dance studio will lend you a room. Any uncluttered space large enough to accommodate your unit will do. Remember, batons in the hands of beginners have little respect for lamps, ashtrays, or other furnishings. You, as organizer of the group, must make the necessary arrangements for the space you will need for the time you will use it.

The group must also understand that hard work, coopera-
tion, and loyalty are necessary if they are to produce a good
unit. Each member must contribute to the group effort
and must be willing to give the required time to lessons and
practice. Pride in the unit's accomplishments and success
must be developed to the extent that nothing interferes with
practice and progress. In a word, each individual must be
dedicated.

Keep your standards high if you wish to develop a first-
class unit. Girls interested only in parade work and performances soon find that the hours of sweat and toil required
to achieve basic skills take away much of the anticipated
glamor, and, in most cases, they soon drop out.

The size of your group depends on you or on the response
to your announcement. Don't be discouraged if at your first
meeting there is a small turnout. It usually happens after
you are organized and trained and have gained publicity
through performances that you will have a long waiting list
of girls wishing to join.

If you recruit a large group, all those interested can be
used. If you prefer to start with a small unit, then you have
to go through a process of elimination.

The kind of group you want to develop also depends on
you—you may want all tall girls, or all short girls, or a combination. In making your choice, remember good health is
necessary, and a trim figure and pretty legs are important.
Age is not a deciding factor for even quite young children can
readily learn wrist action, coordination, and body control.
Ability of the group to work together is essential.

It is advisable if you are choosing a small group that you
select a number of alternates. For example, in a group of nine,
it is wise to have four alternates to protect against loss caused
by illness or resignation. With trained alternates available
you are always able to maintain your schedule—whether of
classes or performances. Alternates should not be considered
as substitutes to be used only when you need them. They are
an integral part of the group and should be included in
every lesson and practice session. Later, in actual performance, they can often be utilized in various ways: as flag bear-

ers or as participants when routines require a larger number of performers.

Your group selected, your lesson schedule and meeting place arranged, you are ready to start. The whole unit begins with the basic figures. This is true even if you have been fortunate enough to find a complete group with past experience. Practice basics as a unit until every baton is moving as one. All movements must be precise and identical—arms and legs moving in perfect unison to the same exact heights. Each member must work toward group perfection because there is no place for individualism in group twirling. Although your unit may contain one or more trained twirlers, they still must drill with the group on basics in order to develop absolute precision. Group work without precision is like a parade without a band.

As I said above, no individual ever tries to excel or outtwirl the others. The accent is on togetherness, and this takes time to attain. Add to interest and enthusiasm mentioned before, team work and patience and you have the ingredients for a successful unit.

Group work is a great deal of fun, and you will find that there is much to be learned from members of the unit. The ideas and suggestions that they present not only benefit the whole unit but also help to sustain individual interest. Don't let the group become bored, and keep lessons and practice sessions happy and lively. Even though the work sometimes seems difficult or tiring or repetitious, to achieve success you must maintain an attitude of enthusiasm. Your own feelings are contagious and obvious, and, if your interest flags, the unit will sense this immediately. Furthermore, a pleasant atmosphere produces a happy group, and an audience senses this at once during a performance.

In working with a variety of personalities it is normal that problems affecting the unit will arise. These should be discussed frankly and openly with the entire group. Every member should expect fair treatment and should speak up if she feels that she is being slighted or overworked. Each member should be able to accept the group's decision. Helpful criticism, given in a tactful manner, should never be resented.

You will find that by settling petty differences in this manner, there will be a minimum of personality clashes and resentment. If there is ever a criticism of a very personal nature, you, as organizer, must handle this confidentially with the member concerned.

Consideration and kindness are necessary for pleasant relations, but, without firmness, lessons and practice will become lackadaisical and undisciplined. You do not have to be a "Simon Legree" to make your group realize you are firm in your decisions. If this fact is established at the beginning, you should have a well-organized and happy unit.

It is most important to clarify your policy on absenteeism. In group work with schedules planned well in advance, only illness, unavoidable medical or dental appointments, or similar emergencies are acceptable excuses. Members who flaunt or ignore the rules should be dropped for the good of the unit. Occasionally, of course, a situation will occur which causes a member to be absent. This should be given consideration, but it should not become a frequent happening.

To summarize, be firm but not stubborn, keep an open mind and accept sincere suggestions, but once you have made a decision, stick to it!

As soon as your group is organized and lessons under way, the marching unit should choose its name. This is not as easy as you might think. The name should be short, catchy, and easy to remember. It should look well on programs and be eye-catching on billboards and marquees. If you have a sponsor, your name should be related to that organization. Usually, a sponsor does not insist on a particular name but wants there to be an association in the public mind.

In Japan one of our most popular marching and twirling groups, which represented an air force base and was sponsored by a fighter squadron, was called the Jet-ettes. This name was appropriate, short, described the sponsor, and also implied that our twirling was accomplished with the speed of a jet. Another foreign group I developed called themselves the Diplomats. Although this group was not sponsored, they did a lot of goodwill work, and the name was most suitable.

Try to be original in your name selection, and do not copy other marching groups' names. A short, clever, imaginative name catches the attention and fixes itself in the memory of the public. Once the group is named, it should always be referred to by its chosen name. Practice is no longer called baton practice. Using the names I mentioned above as examples, it would be called Jet-ettes' practice or Diplomats' practice. This gives your unit its first publicity, and the name is brought to the attention of many people when you talk about your practise.

When the group has completed basics and gone on to more difficult twirling and is marching with perfect precision, it is time to choose your leader or drum majorette. This is usually done by group vote. Your leader is not necessarily the best twirler. She does not have to be. She must, however, be one who can accept responsibility and who is mature enough not to have her head turned by being chosen. Personality and the ability to cooperate with others are important factors in selecting a leader. Other necessary qualities are patience, understanding, tact, conscientiousness, and, of course, enthusiasm.

The choice of the right leader is very important, and should not be placed on a "best friend" basis. The person who will make the most impressive leader should receive your vote because the group is only as good as its leader, and an outstanding leader means an outstanding unit.

If you do not have a sponsor and you feel that the group needs guidance and advice, you may seek these from a number of people: the bandmaster at school, the physical education teacher, or your community youth leader, to name a few. In some areas there are baton schools, and, whether or not you are a student of that school, you will find them willing to offer helpful suggestions.

Very few marching units are fortunate enough to have a band to play for them at practices and lessons. Music, of course, is as important as your batons so you must make arrangements to obtain it. You might engage a drummer, or a pianist, or use records or tape. It is often possible to recruit members of a school band. To achieve the necessary standards for performing publicly, you must practice to music *after* you have mastered basic twirling. It is your responsibility as organizer to provide this essential ingredient in one form or another.

Once your leader is chosen, she should immediately take her place at the front of the unit during practice and lessons, and the group must learn to follow her signals. Members must be patient and understanding and should not expect their leader to be perfect at the beginning sessions.

When you have completed basics, when your group is twirling and marching in perfect unison, when your leader is giving signals smartly, and when you are properly and completely uniformed, you are ready for that first performance. "Where do we perform?" is the next question.

This is easily answered. You will be welcomed by most program chairmen of local associations such as the P.T.A., women's clubs, or civic organizations. A simple letter stating that the (your group name) would enjoy performing and giving full details of your program will result in invitations to start you on your twirling career. Watch the newspapers for listings of talent shows, auditions, amateur shows, and festivals taking place in your area. Write or call the person in charge for information on entering your unit. Parades, usually planned well in advance, often need a baton group, and the chamber of commerce can provide advance information on them. If a band is not provided in the parade, a loudspeaker and tape or records in an accompanying automobile or a hired drummer will serve adequately.

If you are invited to perform indoors, it is necessary to find out in advance how much space you will have to work in. Although a large area is always preferable, you must learn to adjust to smaller spaces and arrange routines accordingly. Always find out exactly how much time will be allotted to your unit, and *never* go over the limit unless it is by popular demand. Programs are usually carefully timed, and an act that exceeds its limit causes confusion. If you are called back for an encore, do not wear out your welcome. Go into your number quickly, accept your applause graciously, and leave your audience feeling they would like to see even more of your skills.

Whenever your group is a part of a scheduled program, be prompt for rehearsals and show consideration to other members of the cast. If musicians accompany your unit, be certain they are thanked for their efforts. Be sure that all group members arrive promptly with all their equipment in good order. Remember—whether the audience is small or large—always try your hardest to put on the best possible show. These people have come to watch you entertain: don't let them down!

If your group is a large one, you may wish to establish several ranks. In addition to the leader or drum majorette, you might have some majorettes, a twirler leader, as well as the baton corps. The drum majorette or leader is at the head of the entire group and is responsible for signaling and guiding all members. The majorettes, usually two or four, are placed right behind the leader, and their routine is different from that of the corps. Leading the baton corps is the twirler-leader who guides the twirlers through their routines. She does not signal and she too follows the drum majorette's signaling. The girls selected for these various ranks are usually chosen by group vote. Their uniforms are sometimes different in style or in color—another decision made by group vote.

A sponsor can be a great help to a marching group just as the baton twirlers can bring useful and favorable publicity to the sponsor. Some of the benefits derived from a sponsor are financial aid, provision of music and practice hall, and publicity and promotion. If sponsors provide uniforms, they have the right to choose the styles and colors. They also have the right to arrange performance schedules.

It is sometimes difficult in the beginning for a newly organized group to find a sponsor, but do not let this dampen your spirits. Your unit may sponsor itself until it has built up publicity by its excellent performances, and then it is likely there will be many offers of sponsorship. Even without a sponsor, your group may participate in any activities in which sponsored groups take part.

Now organized and having learned a bit about the ways of going about securing performance dates, a few brief words are needed *before* you twirl.

2

Before You Twirl

WEARING apparel for the beginner is almost as important as the baton itself. Your body must be free for action, and anything that might interfere with arm or leg movement will hinder progress. Long, full sleeves, crinoline petticoats, full skirts, slippery shoes, full-legged slacks, or bulky shorts are strictly taboo. The ideal costume for baton practice and lessons is the leotard worn by dancers. Though clinging, it has sufficient elasticity to permit adequate freedom of motion and it will never interfere with your baton. Second choice would be slim, comfortable-fitting shorts with a sleeveless or short-sleeved blouse. Slacks may be used but you will find that they are confining when you attempt leg work.

Whatever you choose (or your teacher chooses for you), should be easily maintained. Learning baton twirling requires a great deal of physical effort, mental exertion and, of course, time, so practice garments should be simple to launder and to keep fresh.

The most suitable footwear for the beginner is either tennis shoes or ballet slippers. With a light-weight shoe, it is less difficult for you to perfect kicks and leg raises, and to develop the arched foot. Heavy majorette boots are not recommended while you are going through the learner phase.

Although long hair is pretty, especially during a performance, it can be very distracting during lessons and practice. I suggest that the hair, if long, be drawn back from the face in a pony tail or braids or secured firmly with bobby pins and barettes.

As with any other craft, good equipment is essential. You must have a properly weighted and balanced baton. And the baton must fit the student. The proper length is obtained by measuring from the armpit, the arm held in a horizontal position, to the tip of the middle finger. Most manufacturers make their batons in even inches. If your arm length measures 23″ you would be wise to buy a 24″ baton. Almost any music store can order suitable batons.

I prefer the very thin-shaft baton, and I believe it is better for beginners. More speed with less effort can be obtained, and, since there is less weight, your untrained arm does not tire as quickly. When I have taught in foreign countries where properly weighted batons were not readily available, we managed temporarily with bamboo sticks or broom handles, making sure they were the proper length. I do not advise the use of this equipment for any long period, but you can, if it is necessary, begin with it.

Your baton is a very important piece of equipment and should be given the right care. Its life span in most cases is quite long, and, properly cared for, the shaft will last several years. Leather cases may be purchased for storing and carrying batons, or you may make a cloth case. A piece of material a little longer and wider than the baton is folded in half, stitched up on the open side and one end, and finished with a drawstring closing at the top. The baton should always be kept in its case when not in use.

The rubber ball and tip of the baton are made to take a great deal of use and abuse, but they also need care. Do not pull them off the shaft because this weakens their adhering quality. Constantly removing and replacing the ball and tip might cause either of these pieces to loosen and, during a performance, to go sailing gaily across the room, leaving you to face the audience or judges with a shaft minus one of its important parts. The tip and ball will, in all probability, wear out before the shaft. They receive a lot of wear because of frequent drops from the untrained hands of beginners. When you find the shaft peeking through small holes in the tip or ball, it is time to replace. These replacements may be purchased from the music store or dealer where you bought your baton. The shaft, although durably constructed, may also meet with misfortune. A high toss that you miss may land on a cement curb or pavement or a protruding rock. A collision with another baton can dent the shaft beyond repair. Any extra weight on the shaft can be harmful too: sitting on the baton, or placing it carelessly where a bicycle or auto can run over it. As you handle the baton, you will find that the once-white ball and tip quickly turn an ugly gray-white color. This is easily remedied by washing the ball and tip in warm soapy water, or, if the stains are persistent, by using a strong cleaning powder such as Bab-o or Ajax. Clean the tip and ball regularly. Never wait until the night before a performance. Accumulated dirt and stains are much more difficult to remove. The pride you have in your baton is reflected by its condition when you twirl it. The silver shaft holds its shine, but, to add lustre and sparkle, a quick going-over with silver polish enhances its gleam.

Have a special place to store your baton in its case when not in use. Keep it in an upright position to insure that heavy objects are not placed on it. A corner of a closet is ideal. Countless minutes will be saved if you develop the habit of always returning your baton to its designated place.

Batons look very much alike, and, if you are studying with a large group whose batons were ordered from the same manufacturer, I suggest that you mark your baton in a manner that you can easily identify. There are many ways of doing this, but be sure to keep your mark small and obscure so it will not detract from the baton's appearance. A small speck of nail polish at the base of the ball, or a tiny strip of adhesive tape with your initials on it near the tip, or your initials lightly engraved on the shaft, are some of the usual ways. Your baton is as important to you as her ballet slippers are to Margot Fonteyn. It is a tool in your hand, and its condition reflects the interest and skill of its handler.

Practice clothes and baton all squared away, we must now consider your fitness to begin twirling. As a preliminary conditioning for actual baton lessons, there are three essential exercises which are performed on the floor. To perfect your posture, develop more limber body muscles, strengthen leg muscles, and add grace to your footwork and baton twirling, the Rock, the Peek, and the Leg Raises should be mastered and practiced. The dedicated student will set aside a daily period for these, and every twirler should perform these exercises at least three times a week, allowing not less than five minutes for each exercise. While you do spend some time in class on exercise, weekly lesson time alone is not sufficient to really limber the body.

THE ROCK

Let's start with the Rock. This helps to tighten the stomach muscles as well as to strengthen back muscles. Floor exercises are a must in developing proper posture, most important to a twirler, and help prevent the development of that unattractive, unhealthy, sway-back look.

1) Lie on the floor on your tummy.

2) Bring your legs up, bending your knees.

3) Raise your head and chest up high off the floor.

4) Place the palms of your hands flat on the floor near your waist.

5) With your palms push your chest and shoulders back.

6) Relax your arms and let your body roll forward, raising your knees high off the floor and lowering your chest and tummy to the floor.

7) Keep your head turned to the left or right so that you do not bump your chin.

Repeat, pushing your body up with your palms and relaxing your arms until you are rocking like a rocking chair.

THE PEEK

The Peek helps to strengthen the ankles, develops the arched foot, tightens tummy muscles, and strengthens back muscles.

1) Lie flat on your back with both arms straight along your sides.

2) With your legs stiff and straight, point your toes down,

your feet highly arched. The only parts of your body that move are your head and feet.

3) Raise your head from the floor and at the same time bring your toes up quickly and peek at them. Do not raise your shoulders and do not bend your knees.

4) Hold this position for a few seconds.

5) Lower the head and feet to the floor, keeping your toes pointed and feeling a good arch in your feet.

LEG RAISES

Leg Raises limber your legs, arch your feet, and build endurance for parade work. Use the same body position as in the Peek.

1) Slowly raise your right leg as high as you can, keeping both legs very stiff, your feet arched, and body and head flat on the floor. Do not bend either knee.

2) Slowly lower your leg to its original position.

3) Repeat with the left leg.

In the beginning, do not overdo any of these exercises. Increase exercise time gradually because in this way your endurance builds up and your muscles strengthen.

As the old saying goes, practice makes perfect and only with practice can you develop your skill. It is wiser to practice daily even though it be for a short period of time than to over-exert one day and then neglect practice for several days. The morning, when the body and mind are rested and fresh, is, of course, the best time for exercise.

The following schedule, set for a 15-minute daily period, will help you master the first part of basic baton twirling:

1) Floor exercises—5 minutes

2) Basic Pinwheels, Figure Eights, and Flats, using both right and left arms—5 minutes

3) Variations of the basics, both right and left arms—5 minutes

After your skill develops, add snappy march music to practice sessions. Various routines, set forth later in this book, are excellent for such practice. When your endurance and coordination improve, you will be able to increase practice time, for you will find your arms do not tire as quickly.

At the first group meeting, assign each girl to a specific position, allowing plenty of space for arm and leg motion as well as baton movement. These positions are not necessarily permanent, but could be maintained for the first three lessons to instill discipline and a sense of organization. You may find changes necessary from time to time as problems develop.

Now is the perfect moment to demonstrate correct posture: head high, chin up, shoulders erect, tummy in, and the weight evenly placed on the balls of the feet which are held close together, toes straight ahead.

The following teaching format will guide you through the beginner's stage. This plan is flexible for you must remember that each group will have different problems. Often one unit will grasp a particular twirl very quickly while another may have to spend much practice and extra lessons on this same phase.

Lesson time is 45 minutes, and it is important to stress that the entire period is devoted to learning. Students should be dressed and ready for their lesson at the time class starts. They should have had their drinks of water and attended to all personal necessities so that once instruction commences there are no interruptions.

At the beginning of the first lesson you should explain the meaning of baton twirling, the wrist motion, the baton, and what you expect from your pupils. It is important to let them know you insist on progress and that you will not tolerate any nonsense in the classroom. Your first three lessons should consist of:

1) Floor exercises—5 minutes
2) Basis Pinwheels, Figure Eights, and Flats using both right and left arms—20 minutes
3) Variations of basics—15 minutes
4) Baton salute—5 minutes

Baton Salute is a means of dismissing the class, a way of saying thank you for a good lesson by both teacher and students.

No music is needed for the first three lessons. Pupils will find it impossible to keep up with the music beats until they have developed speed in their twirling.

The three basics and their variations should be mastered with speed and style by the end of the third lesson. After this, music may be used for previously learned work. Never introduce music until the twirls are being executed with speed and grace. Any march music may be used. Each of us has our favorites. I find that the bouncy, standard marches, melodies the students are familiar with, produce best results in the beginner classes.

When the first three lessons are behind you, the following format can be followed:

1) Floor exercises—5 minutes
2) Warm-up session using beginner basics, Pinwheels, Figure Eights, Flats and their variations, with music—5 minutes
3) Review of previous twirls, with music—10 minutes
4) New work, no music—15 minutes
6) Routines or drills, with music—10 minutes
6) Baton Salute

After the group has become proficient and has learned many different twirls, it is wise to devote one lesson out of every ten to a complete review, starting with the first twirl and progressing to the most recently mastered.

Basic Baton Twirls

IT MAY surprise you to learn that baton action is accomplished with a wrist motion. A limber wrist is an asset to the beginner, but, for those not so blessed, rest assured that it will soon develop.

The three most important words as you start baton twirling are (1) the ball, (2) the shaft, and (3) the tip.

Pick up the baton in your right hand, thumb to the ball, grasping the baton in the middle of the shaft. It is held between the thumb and the palm, and your fingers curl around the shaft with your arm dropped in a relaxed position at your right side. Place your left hand on your hip, pull in the tummy, hold your shoulders back, place your feet close together, and begin with the Pinwheel (Figure 1).

PINWHEEL

1) A downward wrist motion brings the tip up on the outside of the arm, the elbow straight.

2) As the palm turns up and away from the body, an inward wrist motion brings the ball up inside and under the arm. The elbow bends slightly as the ball come between the arm and the body.

3) A downward wrist motion dips the ball down, pointing toward the floor while the tip comes up, again outside the arm.

As a beginner, you will find that you are either using excessive elbow motion because of an unlimber wrist or that

1. Pinwheel. Steps 1, 2, and 3.

you are getting bruises as the ball passes up under your arm. Muscles are not yet coordinated, and, as you bring the ball up, you twist the elbow too fast. If you hold the baton in the middle of the shaft and do not let it slip, you will find that you can manipulate it with greater ease.

At first you will grasp the baton too tightly. This prevents relaxed spins. As the wrist limbers and coordination develops, the tight grasp, along with the bruises, will disappear.

The Pinwheel, besides being a basic twirl, is also a wonderful wrist exercise and prepares you for the next stop in baton work.

You must learn to use both the right and left wrists, and, since in the beginning the untrained arm tires quickly, alternate your arms from the very first lesson.

Unless you happen to be left-handed or ambidextrous, you will find your left wrist very awkward. In fact, right now,

2. Figure Eight. Steps 2, 3, and 4.

you are probably finding both left and right hands awkward. This feeling will soon vanish as those tiny tendons and muscles become more responsive.

FIGURE EIGHT

The next basic twirl is the Figure Eight and the name describes the twirl perfectly. We literally "make" a figure eight with the baton (Figure 2).

1) Hold the baton in the right hand, thumb to the ball, in a waist high position.

2) Dip the ball down in front of the body below the waist.

3) The palm of the hand turns in toward the body as you bring the ball of the baton up to a nose high position. The baton is now in a straight up and down position.

4) By turning the palm upward, this motion brings the

tip up to nose high position and pushes the ball straight out away from the body.

5) The wrist rolls out to the right, palm up, which turns the tip out and to the left of the body.

6) Turn the palm down. The ball is pointing front and the tip is pointing back. You are in starting position to go into Step 2 above.

You might think to yourself: dip ball, up ball, up tip, turn out tip. You are "making" the figure eight, and, as your wrist limbers, you will find that you use less elbow motion, less exaggerated arm motion, and that you are developing a nice smooth twirl.

Before proceeding with your next basic, it would be wise to practice the Pinwheel and Figure Eight combinations. With your right hand do four Pinwheels. Next go into four Figure Eights. At first you will note a definite pause as you change from one twirl to another. However, with continued practice you will be able to change twirls speedily and smoothly. Remember to repeat each exercise with your left hand.

The beginner must keep in mind that when one hand is not in use or in a posed position (about which you will learn later), it is always placed smartly on the hip. There is nothing less attractive than an awkward, dangling arm, and, in competitions, you are marked down considerably for this. It is important to develop correct techniques from the beginning and to avoid acquiring bad habits that must be "unlearned" at a later date.

FLAT

The third basic is the Flat and this, like the Figure Eight, describes itself. All the time the baton is in motion, it stays in a flat, horizontal position (Figure 3).

1) The baton is held with thumb to the ball with the right arm at a shoulder high position, extending horizontally to the right.

2) A backward, palm up wrist motion brings the ball to the top of the arm, the elbow bending slightly.

3) The wrist motion continues to roll back and, in a circu-

3. Flat. Steps 1 and 3.

lar motion, starts to roll forward, bringing the tip under the arm. The elbow straightens.

4) The palm turns down and to the left, placing the ball again in position to be brought back over the top of the arm.

All this is accomplished with a backward, rolling, circular wrist motion. The elbow bends and then straightens. You will find that the arm tires quickly when you first start the Flat. As the right arm tires, repeat this twirl with the left. Keep the arm high and the body straight. Good body posture is always important, and it is essential that you keep this in mind.

The three basic twirls, Pinwheels, Figure Eights, and Flats, will develop your wrist motion as well as teach you fundamental techniques. You will learn that there are many variations of these basics, and it will take time to perfect them. Doing these basics with the variations relieves the monotony

4. Pinwheel Up and Down. Steps 2, 3, and 4.

of repeating the same thing over and over. In the variations, baton action is the same, but body and arm placements result in a different appearance of the twirls.

VARIATIONS

After you have developed the Pinwheel to the point where the ball is passing inside and the tip outside the arm with speed and only a few elbow bumps, you may attempt these variations. Let's start with the Pinwheel Up and Down (Figure 4).

PINWHEEL UP AND DOWN

1) Start as you would normally begin the basic Pinwheel and execute several until your baton is spinning with speed.

2) Slowly extend your arm above your head, keeping the baton spinning in Pinwheel motion.

3) Bring the extended arm down to waist position, still Pinwheeling.

4) Bend forward slightly from the waist and bring the arm down to the calf of your right leg, continuing the Pinwheel.

5) Bring the arm again to waist high position, Pinwheeling.

6) Stretch the arm again, high above the head, doing Pinwheels.

The forward wrist motion keeps the baton in Pinwheel motion, and, although the arm movement is slow, the wrist action is fast. You execute many Pinwheels as you move the arm up above the head and down to the calf of your leg. As your right arm tires, shift to the left hand and repeat.

PINWHEEL FRONT AND BACK

Another variation is the Pinwheel Front and Back which goes like this:

1) Start the Pinwheel at waist position.

2) As the baton executes its Pinwheel spins, bring your arm forward to a shoulder high position.

3) Bring your arm back to waist position, still Pinwheeling.

4) Continuing the Pinwheel motion, push your arm to the back.

5) Return your arm to waist position and repeat.

Remember, you keep the baton in motion with the Pinwheel twirl. Your arm in Step 3 is slightly below the waist. Keep your body straight, and be sure not to lean forward or backward with your arm motion.

FIGURE EIGHT HAND CHANGE

There are numerous Figure Eight variations which, you will discover, play a very important part in advanced twirling. It is essential to perfect basic twirls in order to accomplish more advanced twirling techniques.

For the beginner, a good Figure Eight variation is the Figure Eight Hand Change. Using the dip, up, up, and out motion already explained, start with your right hand and complete two Figure Eights.

5. Figure Eight Under the Leg. Steps 1, 2, and 3.

1) On the third dip of the ball, pass the baton, ball leading, in front of the waist to the left side of the body.

2) With the left hand take the baton, thumb to the ball, palm down, and execute two Figure Eights.

3) On the third dip, pass the baton, ball leading, to the right side of the body.

4) The right hand grasps the baton, thumb to the ball, palm down, and repeats the exercise.

After you develop speed, do this exercise with only one Figure Eight in each hand making a smooth change on the second dip.

FIGURE EIGHT UNDER THE LEG

A third variation that you will enjoy is the Figure Eight Under the Leg (Figures 5). Start in the same way as the Figure Eight Hand Change.

1) On the third dip of the ball, pass the baton, ball leading, under the raised right leg. The toe points down. The left leg is locked stiff and tight.

2) The left hand reaches to the right and takes the baton in the center of the shaft, thumb to the ball, palm up, from under the raised right leg.

3) As the left hand executes two Figure Eights, your right leg is lowered to the floor.

4) On the third dip, pass the baton under the raised left leg, repeating Step 2 with the right hand.

5) Repeat Step 3, returning your left leg to the floor and using the right hand to execute the twirl.

Repeat from right to left and, as speed develops, do only one Figure Eight, dipping the baton under your leg on the second dip. Keep body position correct. If your shoulders lean forward as you dip the baton under the raised leg, you will look like a contortionist. If your foot is not arched prettily and pointing to the floor, your leg work will appear grotesque. If the knee of the leg standing on the floor is bent and not in a stiff, locked position, you will seem to be losing your balance.

Although it is wrist motion that keeps the baton spinning, proper body motion and posture are essential if you are to develop technique and style. Without correct body stance, the best baton twirling technique is lost on the audience, judges, or fellow twirlers.

FLAT FROM SIDE TO SIDE

A striking and showy Flat variation is the Flat from Side to Side (Figure 6). Because of the high, extended arm position required while performing this variation, you will find that your arm tires quickly. Don't feel discouraged for in time the muscles become more coordinated and stronger, and a greater endurance develops.

1) Start the Flat in normal position. As your baton gains speed, bring the extended arm to the front center of the body, spinning Flats.

2) Push the arm to the left of your body, continuing Flats.

6. Flat from Side to Side. From the center position, you move first to one side and then the other and repeat this swinging movement.

3) Return the arm from left side across the front to the starting position, twirling Flats.

Be sure to keep the Flats spinning as you change your arm position. You will notice again excessive elbow bending at first, but this, too, is corrected by practice. Although there is always a slight bend of the elbow, the accent is on wrist action. As the arm position changes from the beginning position to the front and side positions, it is necessary to extend the arm as far from the body as possible. The Flat is much prettier and more effective when the arm is held at almost shoulder height. As your arm tires, you will tend to lower your arm position. This is a bad habit, easily developed. Therefore, as soon as the right arm tires, shift to the left. I cannot stress too strongly the importance of acquiring good habits and techniques while learning.

You have now learned three basics and five variations. In order to develop rhythm in twirling and smoothness in movements, I am setting a basic baton routine for you. By this time you should be twirling with speed and be ready to try with music. Not only does practice to music provide inspiration, it also develops that important ability of recognizing music breaks and the speed of the drum cadence.

This routine is set to the bouncy Sousa march, "Stars and Stripes Forever." Playing time (and twirling time) is 3 minutes and 28 seconds. If you do not have a recording of this march, the routine will fit nicely to almost any standard march.

To keep you on the beat in a simple and easy manner, I use a quick 1–2–3–4–5–6–7–8 count. There will be a total of 56 of these 8-counts in the routine. I suggest you first play the music and mentally go through the count before actually trying it.

First two 8-counts. Stand with baton under the right arm. Left hand on left hip. Shoulders back, tummy pulled in, head held high and proud. Remember, when not in use or in a posed position, the hand is on the hip.

1) Pinwheels. Do to four 8-counts.

2) Figure Eights. Do to four 8-counts.

3) Flats. Do to four 8-counts.

4) Figure Eight Hand Changes from right to left hand. Do to six 8-counts. (Note: This twirl is placed here to give you an opportunity to rest your right arm. Baton returns to right hand for Step 5).

5) Flats from Side to Side. Do to four 8-counts.

6) Pinwheels Up and Down. Do to four 8-counts.

7) Figure Eights Under Leg. Do to four 8-counts.

8) Pinwheels Front and Back. Do to two 8-counts.

9) Figure Eights. Do to four 8-counts.

10) Flats from Side to Side. Do to four 8-counts.

11) Pinwheels. Do to four 8-counts.

12) Figure Eight Hand Changes. Do to two 8-counts.

13) Flats. Do to four 8-counts.

14) Pinwheels Up and Down. Do to four 8-counts.

15) Baton returns to under arm in starting position.

I have made this routine simple with uniformity in the count to enable you to concentrate on twirl changes and music breaks. You will notice that the count is quick. The music may confuse you at first for you are concentrating on several things at the same time. As you continue to practice, you will find that the baton spins faster, and, subconsciously, your mind will carry the cadence, relieving you of count concentration.

As I said before, appearance of twirls can be completely changed by using different arm placement and body motions. For example, when executing a Figure Eight, first raise the arm high above the head, execute the twirl, then drop the arm to the side and repeat the Figure Eight.

Similarly, Flats can take on the appearance of a Cross-Turn: the right leg is crossed in front of the left leg at the ankle, the twirler raises high on the half-toe (commonly called tiptoe), and quickly spins the body around to the left, making a full turn as the arm keeps the baton in a Flat twirl.

There is much to be learned from careful study of this chapter on basic twirls. I want to stress that progress cannot be forced. If your skill on the basics is not fully developed, it is senseless to go on to more complex movements. Study, practice, and review the basic twirls and their variations until you are perfect!

4

Two-Hand Twirls, Stationaries, Poses

To GAIN the coordination needed for Two-Hand Twirls, Stationaries, and Poses, it is essential to learn another floor exercise which will add suppleness and strength to the waist and upper part of your body. Add it to your practice sessions!

WAIST BEND

1) Place knees closely together and kneel.
2) Stretch both arms high toward the ceiling and feel the rib cage pull up.
3) Keep the body tall as you lean slowly to the right, arms stretched full length.
4) Lean as far as you can without sagging.
5) Return to starting position.
6) Lean slowly to the left, repeating Steps 3 and 4.
7) Return to starting position and repeat 6 times.

CARTWHEEL

Now that your wrists are more limber, and this fact has given you confidence, we shall start on basic beginner twirls utilizing both hands for the execution of one twirl. A good one to begin with is the Cartwheel (Figure 7). This should be done with one hand at first to develop speed and grace.

1) Hold baton in Pinwheel position, right hand.
2) Execute one Pinwheel.

7. Cartwheel. Steps 3, 4, and 5.

3) With a forward wrist motion, palm turning up, bring the tip toward the hip.

4) Keeping the palm up, turn the wrist to the right as far as possible. This motion extends the shaft to the right, tip leading, in a horizontal position.

5) Raise the arm high above the head, keeping palm up. The ball now points toward the back of the body, tip toward the front, pointing straight up.

6) With a sweeping motion, bring the arm down to the right side, turning the palm down as you do so.

7) The tip of the baton twirls to point toward the floor, the ball upright. You are again in the Pinwheel position.

You will soon develop graceful, sweeping arm motions. It will help you increase smoothness if you think: Pinwheel, tip in, tip out, arm up, arm down. When perfected, the Cartwheel is a showy twirl. However, you must be careful as always of your body posture. Do not lean with the arm motion, and be sure to keep your torso straight. Now, repeat this twirl with the left hand until you can perform it smoothly. Practice with each hand alternately before trying the combined movement. When you have mastered speedy twirls with each hand, the next phase is simple.

CARTWHEEL WITH RIGHT AND LEFT HANDS

To execute the Cartwheel from right to left hands, proceed as above through Step 4, then:

1) Bring the right arm up to shoulder height with palm up.

2) Turn palm down as you gracefully swing the arm to the front of the body and to the left, tip leading.

3) Stop at waist height on your left side.

4) The left hand grasps the shaft, thumb toward the ball, and the right hand releases.

5) Left arm drops to Pinwheel position at your left side and right hand is placed on hip.

6) Repeat above, starting with left-hand Pinwheel.

While learning this twirl, you will use too much arm movement, but, as speed develops and wrist action predominates, arm motion will become coordinated and graceful.

There are many variations of the Cartwheel: the Double Cartwheel, the Reversed Cartwheel, to name a couple. Naturally it is important to study and master the basic Cartwheel so that the advanced variations can be accomplished easily.

AROUND THE BODY

The next basic two-hand twirl is the Around the Body (Figure 8). This is a versatile twirl, and entire routines can be set on variations of it. Therefore, it is essential that you perfect your ability to perform it.

1) Baton is in the right hand in Figure Eight position, left hand on the hip.

2) Execute one Figure Eight.

3) Dip the ball in back of the body, waist high.

4) Left hand reaches behind the body to grasp the shaft

8. Around the Body. Steps 4, 6, 6, 7, 8, and Reverse Step 3.

in the center, thumb to tip, palm turning away from the body.

5) Right hand releases grip on shaft and is placed on right hip.

6) Left hand brings the baton out on the left side with a forward wrist motion, baton in horizontal position.

7) A backward wrist motion of the left hand, palm turning up, places the tip to the back, ball pointing forward.

8) With a forward wrist motion, palm turning down, the left hand brings the shaft forward in front of the body in a horizontal position over the head.

9) The right hand grasps the shaft, thumb to the ball, in this position.

10) Left hand releases and is placed on the hip. You are now ready to start again with the Figure Eight, using the right hand.

To develop a smooth rhythm, repeat mentally: Figure Eight and dip and out, back, front. As speed increases the baton will give the illusion of making a complete circle around your body.

This twirl and its variations are excellent for parade work. There is little chance of drops, and the bright sunlight gleaming on the shaft is most effective. Furthermore, this is a restful twirl. Because you are using both arms equally, it gives an opportunity to rest the usually overworked right arm. As you become more relaxed and more expert in twirling, and arm motions are not so accented you will find that the Around the Body and its variations are most enjoyable.

AROUND THE BODY REVERSE

The Around the Body Reverse is an interesting twist on this basic twirl. Here we do exactly what the twirl describes: reverse our motion at a certain stage of its execution.

1) Perform the above Around the Body through Step 7.

2) Using a forward wrist motion, palm turning down, bring the tip front with the left hand.

3) With the tip leading, push the shaft behind the body at waist level (Figure 8).

4) The right hand, palm up and turning away from the body, takes the shaft in back of the body, thumb to the ball.

5) The right hand brings the shaft out from its waist high position and sweeps into a Figure Eight.

The mental count for the Reverse is: Figure Eight and dip, and out, back, dip back.

A fascinating twirl and a wonderful exercise can be performed by doing one Around the Body and one Around the Body Reversed. Let's try it. Subconsciously you are saying: Figure Eight and dip and out, back, front. Figure Eight and dip and out, back, dip back. Do it slowly at first. Don't try for speed in new twirls. This comes with practice. In most cases if the beginner concentrates on speed instead of perfection, it is easy to leave out one small step, one small wrist motion, or one arm motion, all of which naturally lead to confusion. The wrist and arm motion must follow exactly the pattern I have explained to create the perfect twirl. Try not to be impatient because in a very short time speed will develop, wrists and arms will move gracefully, and you will be doing what you have learned the RIGHT WAY.

As you continue to learn additional twirls you must never neglect basics. Each basic is important and has its place in baton routines. A student who neglects any of them, feeling they have now become too simple, will regret it. With ease comes grace and with practice comes perfection. It is more pleasing to watch a performance of simple basic twirls done perfectly than to observe a student attempt difficult twirls with elbows protruding, knees bent, body distorted. If, in the beginning, you concentrate on proper posture and correct holding of the baton, you develop a feeling for the right stance and arm movement. This helps as you go on to intermediate and advanced twirling.

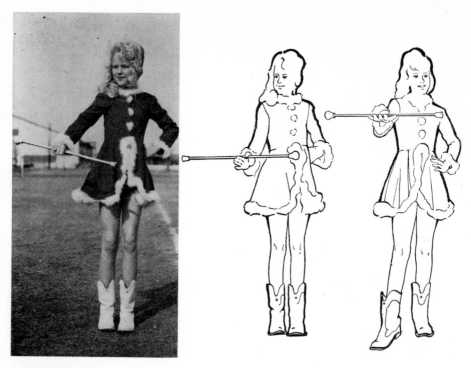

9. Hand Roll. Steps 1, 3, and 5.

HAND ROLL

The Hand Roll (Figure 9) is most difficult for the beginner, and we tackle this twirl with determination for without it we cannot progress into High Aerials and Partner Pitches. It describes itself: the baton actually rolls around the hand. While doing this twirl, your mental count is: roll and grab, roll and grab.

1) Pick up the baton in the right hand, palm down and thumb pointing toward the *tip*. Left hand is on hip.

2) The shaft of the baton is held in front of the body about waist high.

3) A backward wrist motion rolls the shaft back between the thumb and first finger. Tip points to the right, ball to the left.

4) The shaft is released from the thumb and first finger.

5) The palm is reversed and turns down, forcing the shaft to roll over the top of the hand.

6) With palm down, quickly grab the shaft with the right hand, thumb to tip, after it has completed Step 5.

7) The baton is back in starting position.

This twirl requires quick action. You will probably find that your wrist coordination is not fast enough. As the baton passes off the hand and you execute the "grab" with thumb toward the tip, the shaft often rolls so fast that you are grasping thin air while the baton bounces on the floor. This is to be expected at first, so don't be discouraged. After a few tries you will be catching some of them, and before long it will become as easy as the Pinwheel is for you now!

The Hand Roll *must* be perfected with both hands. After you have tired the right arm, switch to the left. It will feel more awkward at first, and you will find the left arm takes longer to perfect.

HAND ROLL WITH PASS BACK

A good practice exercise as well as a good twirl is a variation of the Hand Roll utilizing both hands with a Pass Back.

1) Execute one Hand Roll with right hand.

2) After the grab, pass the shaft, ball leading, to the back of the body at waist height.

3) Grasp the shaft in back of the body with left hand, thumb to tip.

4) Using a sweeping motion, bring the baton from the back of the body to the left side and to the front of the body at waist height.

5) Execute a Hand Roll with the left hand. Repeat Steps 2, 3, and 4, releasing from the left hand to the right hand.

As you repeat from right to left, the mental count is: roll, grab, push back, bring front.

HAND ROLL WITH NECK PUSH AROUND

Another variation of the Hand Roll is the Neck Push Around (Figure 10). This really takes coordination! The mind must control the body, and wrists and arms must be agile.

10. Hand Roll with Neck Push Around. Step 7.

1) Execute one Hand Roll with the right hand, catching the baton near the end of the shaft, close to the tip.

2) The ball swings down toward the floor as thumb and first finger grasp the shaft.

3) With a sweeping arm motion, swing the ball from its near the floor position to the left side and up, placing the shaft at the back of the neck.

4) The head drops forward slightly.

5) The ball extends beyond the right shoulder.

6) The right elbow is in front of the nose.

7) The left hand comes off the hip, is placed under the right arm, and grasps the baton near the tip end, thumb to the ball and palm down.

8) The right hand releases the baton to the left hand.

9) The left hand brings the baton down to a horizontal position in front of the body, waist high.

10) Execute half a Hand Roll, grabbing with the thumb

pointing to the ball. (To execute half a roll, the shaft passes over the top of the left hand, the tip moving from right to left. In this position the hand very quickly moves from the position under the shaft, pulls in toward the body, and swiftly grabs the shaft on top with thumb to the ball— not the usual Hand Roll position.) Pitch the baton to the right hand.

11) The right hand catches the shaft, thumb to the tip, and is in starting position for Hand Roll.

You must concentrate on placing the shaft in a horizontal position at the back of the neck. If you find that the ball is pointing backwards instead of to the right, take note of your arm. Is it pushed up high under the chin? Are you holding the baton by thumb and first finger? If you are having difficulty grasping the shaft with the left hand, check its position. Is the left arm pushed up tightly under the right arm? Are the elbows straight, not drooping? Is the palm of the left hand facing down? Check all these points and practice, practice, practice!

You and your baton are becoming close friends now and you find you can manipulate it with grace and ease. You are learning each new combination more readily by this time. Your arms have begun to build up strength, endurance, and agility. You feel you are standing properly and grasping that shaft in the right position.

For the beginner, I recommend not practicing in front of a mirror. As you become more skilled, a mirror helps you to develop showmanship and a snappy technique. However, when you are a novice, a mirror does nothing but add confusion.

I am sure you enjoyed the first routine, and, to give a lift to your practice sessions, I am setting forth another which includes all basic twirls and their variations. It is set to the "Colonel Bogey March" in 120 cadence which means 120 beats per minute. If you do not have this music, almost any standard march may be used. We shall use the 8-count again to permit more concentration on the twirls. There will be 35 8-counts:

1) Start with the baton under your arm as you did in the first routine.

2) On the drum roll, hold your pose through the first count of eight.

3) Cartwheel in right hand. Do to two 8-counts.

4) Pinwheel in right hand. Do to one 8-count.

5) Around the Body. Do to two 8-counts.

6) Around the Body Reverse. Do to two 8-counts.

7) Flats in right hand. Do to one 8-count.

8) Flats from Side to Side in right hand. Do to one 8-count.

9) Flats in right hand. Do to one 8-count.

10) Pinwheel Back and Forth in right hand. Do to one 8-count.

11) Figure Eight in right hand. Do to two 8-counts.

12) Figure Eight Change From Right to Left Hand. Do to two 8-counts.

13) Cartwheel Right Hand to Left. Do to one 8-count.

14) Cartwheel Left Hand to Right. Do to one 8-count.

15) Hand Roll and Pass Back. Do to two 8-counts.

16) Hand Roll and Neck Push Around. Complete in one 8-count.

17) Figure Eight in right hand. Do to one 8-count.

18) Figure Eight Under the Leg in right hand. Do to two 8-counts.

19) Cartwheel in right hand. Do to two 8-counts.

20) Around the Body. Do to two 8-counts.

21) Pinwheel Up and Down in right hand. Do to two 8-counts.

22) Hand Roll in right hand. Do to count of 1–2–3–4.

23) Flats in right hand. Do to count of 5–6–7–8.

24) Pinwheel Up and Down in right hand. Do to two 8-counts.

25) Around the Body. Do to one 8-count.

26) Around the Body Reverse. Do to one 8-count.

27) Pose with baton under the arm.

This exercise routine utilizes most of the twirls and introduces a quicker count in a few places. It takes concentration to shift the baton from one hand to the other and to

11. Baton Salute. Note that the arm placement of the center figure is incorrect.

remember the proper place on the shaft to grasp the baton.

By this time you should be developing a feeling for the music, and you can almost tell the routine breaks in twirls by the music. I recommend from now on that practice on these already learned be done to music. You will be surprised how soon the baton motion keeps the rhythm and how easily wrists and arms move with smooth quickness. In a very short time you will have both one-hand and two-hand basics spinning gracefully, and you will feel the twirl change with the music break. Twirling to music is inspiring, entertaining, and puts a lift into your practice sessions.

BATON SALUTE

Now it may seem strange, but all baton work is *not* twirling! There are many impressive Lunges, horizontal flat work, and clever Posing. To rest our arms a bit, let's now take up this phase of baton work.

The Baton Salute (Figure 11) is most important and has specific meaning. It is used to salute our nation's flag and has the same significance as other ceremonial and patriotic salutes. It must always be executed smartly and with great pride. The Baton Salute is also used as a sign of recognition when passing other twirlers, when our national anthem or other national anthems are played, and when passing reviewing stands in parades. You must learn to go into the Salute from almost any baton position. But to simplify learning the Baton Salute, let's try it from a stationary position.

BATON SALUTE FROM STATIONARY POSITION

1) The baton is held under the right arm, ball near eye level and extended front to the right of the face.

2) The thumb and first finger, pointing toward the ball, grasp the shaft just below the ball in the same manner as you would hold a pencil.

3) Left hand is on the hip, and the body is tall and proud.

4) The middle of the shaft is held under the armpit, tip extending to the back.

5) The muscle of the right arm releases the shaft.

6) With a forward wrist motion, the baton is snapped forward to the center of the body, ball near nose height. At this point the baton is in a vertical position, center front of the body, and the action has changed finger position.

7) The right thumb points down to the tip of the baton, palm facing away from the body. The right-hand little finger is on the shaft at the base of the ball. The other fingers curl outward around the shaft.

8) The baton is snapped to a position at the left shoulder, still in a vertical position.

9) The right wrist is now to the left at chin height, right elbow held high and pointing forward.

10) The left hand comes off the hip, palm down, thumb in, and rests above the tip of the baton in a horizontal position. The left elbow bends slightly.

11) The head is turned to the object being saluted.

If you should be executing a twirl at the time it is neces-

12. Baton Salute with a Lunge added.

sary to go into a Salute, quickly get the baton into the right hand in proper position. Variations of the Baton Salute are used during civic and military parades, formal concerts, and at football half-time. The basic salute remains the same, but a Lunge or Split is added (Figure 12). As you practice the Baton Salute, you will find that you snap the shaft in front of your chest in one quick movement as the wrist and fingers simultaneously take their proper positions.

UNDER ARM STATIONARY

Stationary baton positions are used many times in long parades or during long routines. They help rest the arms and are effective when done properly. There are many of these and we'll start with the Under Arm.

1) Pick up the baton in the right hand with the thumb

and first finger holding the shaft near the ball, as you would hold a pencil.

2) The middle of the shaft is between the right arm muscle and the armpit.

3) The tip of the baton points to the back at a downward angle.

4) The ball of the baton is extended forward at nose height, left hand on the hip.

5) With a slight wrist motion, the ball moves to the left, nose high, and to the right, nose high.

As you execute the wrist motion you will notice the right arm up to the bent elbow also moves. The left and right motion is done to the drumbeat or musical rhythm.

EXTENDED RAM STATIONARY

The Extended Arm Stationary is much the same, but the shaft and arm are placed in different positions (Figure 13).

1) Pick up the baton with your right hand, first finger going under the shaft near the ball. The thumb is placed on top of the shaft, palm up.

2) Extend the arm high above the head and turn palm down.

3) The shaft rests on the arm up to the elbow and the tip extends back to the right of the shoulder. Left hand is on the hip or posed.

4) With a slight wrist motion left and right, keep time to the music.

HORIZONTAL STATIONARY

The Horizontal Stationary is restful and always welcome after several minutes of fast twirling. Both hands are used.

1) The right hand is placed on the shaft near the ball with palm down and thumb toward the tip.

2) The left hand is placed near the tip with palm down and thumb toward the ball.

3) The baton is in front of the body at waist height in a horizontal position.

4) With a decided wrist motion left and right, the baton moves snappily from side to side in time to the music.

13. Extended Arm Pose.
(The Extended Arm Stationary is identical except the left leg remains on the ground.)

14. Waist Stationary.

An eye-catching variation of the Horizontal which requires no hand changing on the shaft is the "left, right, up up" motion. After you have done the wrist motion to the right, quickly raise the baton up in front of the nose, palms down, and then with a fast wrist movement bring the baton in its horizontal position up above the head. Drop it quickly down to a left position, keeping time to the music. This variation is later used with Hitch Kicks.

WAIST STATIONARY

The Waist Stationary is truly a stationary position for the baton is not moved at all. This position is used during

15. Drum Major's Stationary.

parades when awards are being presented, or in group work during solo twirling performances (Figure 14).

1) Pick up the baton shaft with the right hand near the ball, palm up, first finger pointing to the ball underneath the shaft, thumb pointing to the ball on top of the shaft.

2) Turn the palm toward the body and bring the ball into the waist at the far right side.

3) The elbow is bent, and the ball rests on the waist.

The elbow should point to the right and the middle of the shaft rests in the arm crease at the elbow, the tip and rest of the shaft extending beyond the elbow. The baton is in diagnoal position.

DRUM MAJOR'S STATIONARY

One of the most difficult Stationaries is the Drum Major's, which appears to be so easy but which takes a tremendous amount of strength and wrist action (Figure 15).

1) Pick up the baton as in the Waist Stationary.

2) Bring the ball in front of the face at nose height.

3) The first few inches of the shaft rest between the thumb and first finger. The wrist and these few inches are all you have to control the baton. The rest of the shaft is high in the air at a diagonal angle.

4) The right arm is bent and the elbow is at shoulder height.

5) A downward thrust of the wrist pushes the ball just below nose level.

6) An upward thrust brings the ball back to nose position.

Only wrist action is used because a swaying arm in this position would be ugly. The angle of the long shaft is most important. It must hold its position and not move from upright to horizontal as you proceed with the movement. There is a slight elbow movement and a slight arm flex as the wrist motion goes up and down to the music beat. The shaft must not droop nor the ball slip down. There are many things to concentrate on when you learn this Stationary, and the arm tires quickly in this position. But in time you develop the "feel," and ball, shaft, tip, wrist, and elbow automatically stay in their proper positions.

During long parades and routines, Stationaries have their place. When performed properly, they are very smart and snappy; they give the twirler a chance to rest tired arms, and thus help to prevent drops. Perhaps you are already planning your own routines. If so, include some Stationaries.

POSING

Posing is another phase of stationary baton work. Although usually we go into a Pose from a twirl or motion, the Pose itself is a complete pause of body, and often of baton, movement. Posing has many purposes and can be used in numerous clever ways. Naturally, at the end of a routine after a performance, a Pose is our way of telling the audience we have completed our work and of thanking them for their attention and applause. At the conclusion of specially difficult twirling, a Pose for judges or audience is recom-

16. Arabesque Pose.   17. Waist Pose.

mended, and often during group routines Posing is most effective.

ABRABESQUE POSE

From ballet we have borrowed the Arabesque Pose. While doing this Pose, a Flat, Pinwheel or Thumb Twirl, is most striking (Figure 16).

1) Lock the right leg in a tight, stiff position.

2) Raise the left leg, foot arched and toe pointed, to an extended high position to the back.

3) Lean the body slightly forward from the waist. Keep the baton in motion as you hold the Arabesque Pose. The right leg must be locked tightly to hold the balance and weight of the body.

WAIST POSE

Although you may go into the Waist Pose (Figure 17) from a number of different twirls, in the beginner stage we will

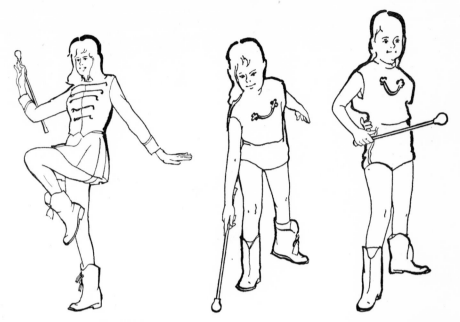

18. Partially Extended
Arm Pose.

19. Lunge Pose.

20. Waist Pull Back
from a Lunge Pose.

start with the Flat twirl. Execute Flat twirls at the far right of
the body to a count of seven:

1) On the eighth count quickly pass the baton to the left
side of the body, ball leading, and bring the middle of the
shaft in to the waist.

2) The left leg comes up with toe pointing down, foot
arched.

3) The left arm extends straight up with fingers together
and palm turned in. Figure 17 shows the twirler facing away
from audience to emphasize baton position. Performers
would face audience.

4) Hold the Pose for a count of one.

5) The left arm returns to hip position, left leg returns
to the floor, and the right arm executes the twirl again.

PARTIALLY EXTENDED ARM POSE

Another showy Pose is the Partially Extended Arm Pose
(Figure 18), which may be done from various twirls. An easy

one to start with is the Pinwheel. Do Pinwheels to a count of seven with the right hand.

1) On the eighth count with a backward wrist motion, flip the tip of the baton back to the elbow.

2) Raise the arm to a partially extended position, elbow bent.

3) Raise the left leg high with toe down and foot arched.

4) Pose the left arm gracefully to the left side.

5) Hold Pose for count of one.

6) Left arm and leg return to normal position and right hand commences the twirl gain.

LUNGE POSE

The Lunge Pose (Figure 19) is decidedly different, and from it we can go into Shoulder Pulls and Body Rolls. As with other Poses, we can do this from various twirls, but for an easy start we will begin with a Hand Roll. As you do the "roll and grab" of the Hand Roll, catch the shaft near the tip with thumb pointing toward the ball.

1) Using a quick body motion, lunge forward on the right foot, bending the knee and placing the ball of the baton on the floor.

2) The left leg extends back in a locked position with the toe turning out slightly to the left.

3) The right arm is straight.

The left arm may be posed to the side of the body or it may be placed at the back of the body, extended far to the right, palm turned away from the body and thumb up in position to catch the shaft as the twirler pulls it back with the right arm to waist position and releases it to the left arm (Figure 20).

MAJORETTE POSE

The Majorette Pose is used often in photographs as well as in routines. I am sure you have seen it many times. We shall go into it from an Around the Body, executed once:

1) Pass the shaft from the left to the right hand with palm facing in.

2) Grasp the baton between thumb and first finger close to the ball, thumb and finger pointing to the ball.

3) Bring the baton to chest height, holding the shaft in a diagonal position.

4) Place the left hand on the hip and raise the left leg high with toe down, foot arched.

The right leg is holding the body weight and must be tightly locked. Shoulders are pulled back, and the right elbow is bent and held high, away from the body. Keep the shaft at a right angle.

Clever Posing is accomplished with quick baton movements as well as with arms and legs. Hand positions are important to complete the picture of the Pose. Practice Poses until you are sure of each movement, and the entire execution is made to a count of one with precision and smoothness.

There are many variations of Poses, and you will probably originate a few of your own as you develop skill in twirling.

By now with your knowledge of the basics and with your keen interest in baton twirling, you should have a sense of accomplishment. Be sure you thoroughly understand all basic twirls, exercises, Stationaries, variations, routines, and Poses before attempting the next phase of baton work.

5

The Strut

As YOU watch with envy the high-stepping Strut of the drum majorette or baton twirler, please remember that this saucy prance has not just happened. Many long hours of practice have been spent in mastering the rhythmic steps and perky body motions as she steps left, right, keeping perfect time to the drum cadence. In addition, she has had to develop the grace of a dancer in body and arm movements, the timing of a musician, and the winning smile of a vote-getting politician.

In every phase of baton work the Strut is of utmost importance. In competitions you are judged on Strutting ability, and in parade work the Strut actually acounts more than twirling. Everyone develops her own individual characteristic style in Strutting. Just as no two personalities are identical, so no two Struts are the same. Physical features affect Strut characteristics. The girl with a long-legged stride certainly does not perform in the same manner as the girl with shorter legs. However, there are two things every strutter must have: proper basic body posture and, most important of all, the ability to keep time with the cadence. The drum or music actually speaks left, right, left, right, and you must hear this and step left, right, left, right, at the proper time.

You will notice in all Poses the left leg is the one that is raised (Figures 16–18). The left leg is the one with which we *always* start marching because the drum or music tells us left first, then right. Nothing will send a bandmaster or drillmaster into a fit of temper faster than a marcher stepping pertly out on her right foot when the drum is beating left.

It is not difficult to keep the beat if you *listen* to the drum. The cadence will vary with different arrangements, but the pronounced left, right, left, right, is there, regardless of the drummer's speed. Before attempting the Strut it would be wise to play march music and step in place to the beat. Listen to the left, right of the drum and mark time with it. As you become skilled at marching, you will find that you *cannot* march off the beat anymore than a piano player can play off key. Eventually you will develop such a sense of timing that your mind and body will revolt if you try to step right when the drum is beating left. This does, however, take time and practice.

STRUT EXERCISE

A preliminary exercise which will help develop your leg work is the Strut Exercise, and this should be practiced to tone up leg muscles before trying actual Strut steps.

1) Stand with body tall and feet together.

2) With the knee bent, slowly bring the left leg up as high as possible without leaning forward, toe pointing down, foot arched.

3) Keep the right leg in locked position.

4) Hold this position for a count of four before slowly returning the leg to floor position, toe first, and snapping the knee back to lock the leg.

5) Repeat with the right leg.

At first your balance will be off, and it will be difficult to hold the pose for a count of four. As coordination develops and balance becomes improved, increase the count to eight. This exercise pulls and limbers the muscles used in the Strut and develops the quick ankle action and leg lock to produce the prance so necessary for a good Strut.

21(left). Strut.

22(right). Strut with left arm swaying back and forth with the drum cadence.

THE STRUT

Now to begin the Strut, let's start with an Extended Arm Stationary baton position (Figures 21–22). The left hand is on the hip and the body is tall and proud.

1) Draw the shoulders back and tilt the chin up slightly.

2) Bring the toe of the left leg up to right knee height, toe down, foot arched.

3) Right leg is on the floor in locked position.

4) As the left foot returns to floor position, step forward, toe first, and bring the heel down with a quick ankle motion, locking the left leg tightly.

5) Raise the right leg up to left knee height and repeat this procedure.

6) Repeat with left and right legs alternately.

Be sure the shoulders are pulled back, the tummy tucked in, and the chin lifted. At this moment you feel about as graceful as a duck, for the knees do not want to stay locked,

the chin automatically droops, and the shoulders hunch forward. The slow motion of your legs as you concentrate makes you feel you are doing a waltz instead of a snappy march. Don't despair for, as with twirling, we must tackle the Strut slowly at first in order to develop correct form.

There are many *don'ts* in Strutting: don't sway your back—hold your shoulders firmly back and erect; don't touch the opposite knee with your toe as you bring the leg up—merely bring that toe to knee height; don't plow your foot down—place it down gently and gracefully, toe first; don't slap the heel on the floor—let the quick ankle action bring the heel down; don't bend the knee of the leg on the floor—keep it stiffly locked; don't let your chin get tilted too high in the sky and push your head back—maintain a perky chin line; don't let your derrière or tummy protrude—keep the tummy tucked in and the seater tucked under. And most important of all—don't give up! In a short time you will have conquered the Strut!

At first practice the Strut slowly. Speed is not essential at this point, and I recommend *no* music at this stage. Perform the Strut as though it were your normal walk. Be sure the legs are raised high, the left hand is on the hip, and the baton does not sag from its original Extended Arm Stationary position.

As I explained in Chapter 2, it is not wise for the beginner to start learning to Strut in majorette boots. You will have difficulty enough without trying to lift a heavy boot gracefully off the floor. Once you have developed a style and have confidence in your Strut, it is time to begin working in boots. Until then ballet slippers or other light footwear are advisable.

To achieve a saucy little body movement so that you don't feel like a high-stepping zombie, let's use the Horizontal Stationary at waist level for the next step in mastering the Strut. As you do your left, right footwork, snap the baton from left to right in this position. This will give you a more relaxed feeling, but do not let it make you feel so relaxed that you lose your proper body posture. Keep in mind that the baton must stay at waist height, and, even though the arms are thrust forward, the shoulders are still pulled back and the chin tilted. After you have mastered the above exercise, try the Strut to music. Music will provide the extra incentive to put more effort into practice. You will find it is easy while practicing to taper off from a high-stepping prance to a Strut similar to an ordinary march. This is a natural tendency, and you are not doing it intentionally. Concentrating as you are on baton, shoulders, and head, you are apt to forget the high leg step. Without the raised leg, there is no style to the Strut. Hence it is most important to pay special attention to leg work.

As soon as you have a feeling for the Strut and are keeping left, right time to the drum using the Stationary baton position, you are ready to commence twirling as you Strut. To begin in an easy manner, start with basic Pinwheels, Figure Eights, and Flats. Maintain your body posture as you twirl. Remember the body stays straight and tall and does not lean from side to side with the twirling wrist and arm motions. Be absolutely sure you have acquired style in your Strut, and that your posture is correct before attempting two-hand twirls. If you rush into these before you are really ready, you'll discover you will have lost all the progress you've made. Movements become awkward and ugly if body position is not maintained. Coordination, as I've said many times before, comes only with practice. It cannot be forced.

As with twirling, endurance must be built up slowly in Strutting. Parades are often long, and at times you may have to march up and down hills, on rough pavements or gravel. Occasionally the weather does not cooperate. Your first few long parades may exhaust you, but after a few months you find that you can keep the pace through almost any type of parade. Until then your legs will feel like wooden stumps, and you will think you cannot take another step. But the parade must go on, and the audience must never know that under that sparkling smile there is leg ache, misery, and tired, tired feet. The spirited band music and the appreciative watchers spur you on, but, for the novice, the time comes when rest must be permitted. In every parade route there are places along the way where you come to a dull spot. Here, perhaps there are very few people and their eyes are on the float which has just passed or they are looking beyond you to the next float. At this time, catch a few minutes' rest by lowering your leg height. You can still keep the Strut snappy and precise by extra body motion and hip sway, but you may rest your legs by ordinary marching steps. Remember, though, this is just for a brief rest and *not* for the remainder of the parade. A few minutes of easy marching gives you a second wind, and you will be able to Strut high until you reach the next dull spot along the route.

The reviewing stand is, of course, one of the high spots of the parade route. Here you must be at your very best. It is customary to use the Baton Salute when passing the reviewing stand, and, regardless of your tiredness, you must Strut in a high, graceful, and handsome style. Cameras are another important feature of the parade route. When you see a camera focused on you, whether newsreel, TV, press, or enthusiastic amateur, you must give your all. You have impressed the cameraman enough for him to want your picture, so co-operate by making it a good one.

The drum beat, the crowd's cheers and applause, the flash bulbs, all make parade work exciting, and you will find you are astonished by your endurance. Your performance will amaze you! As a matter of fact, you can become so elated that you begin to feel you are the only person on parade. Since this, of course, is not so, consideration of the other marching units and floats is most necessary. Show-offs and limelight hoggers are quickly detected and as quickly ignored.

The drum majorette's or leader's signals are your guide, and you must train yourself to pay instant heed to them. Signaling and its importance will be discussed in a later chapter. It is enough to mention here that the leader must be qualified, for the precision of the entire group rests on her, while the precision of your marching is yours alone. Learn to steal quick, frequent glances at the leader and train your ears to listen closely to the whistle signals so that you do not disrupt this precision.

In time you will learn that the best-organized parades will have their problems: motorized floats sometimes break down, forcing a complete halt; spasmodic placing can develop as a parade is en route, necessitating a faster or slower pace; a change of the planned route might occur after the parade is under way; and it is not uncommon for detours to be set up. Your leader must be prepared for any emergency and must be able to signal the group through any change, and you must be able to follow these signals without hesitation.

In competition you are judged and graded on your Strutting ability so you must develop such smooth, rhythmic, graceful movements that there is no appearance of effort in your high-stepping prance.

In stage performances, the eye of the audience is caught by your Strut as much as by your twirling baton. So it is not difficult to see that a good Strut is to your advantage.

6

Leg Work

WELL-DEVELOPED body coordination and wrist motion are essential before beginning leg work. Strut exercises and practice, along with basic Poses and Stationaries, have done much to assist, and you are now moving arms and body with deft sureness which results in faster, smoother twirling. You should be ready to undertake leg work.

Leg work is trick work, and, although not difficult to grasp, it must be practiced until it can be done with tremendous speed. Preliminary exercise again plays an important part. To develop high leg kicks without bending the body at the waist, the following will prove a good start.

HIGH KICKS

1) Stand tall, feet close together. Place both hands on the hips, tummy back, chin up.

2) Pull the elbows back to remind yourself that shoulders must stay back in place.

3) Kick the right leg to the front as high as you can without bending body or knee.

4) Arch the foot so the toe points straight out away from the body.

5) Return to starting position.

6) Kick the right leg straight out to the side, toe pointing out, foot arched.

7) Return to starting position.

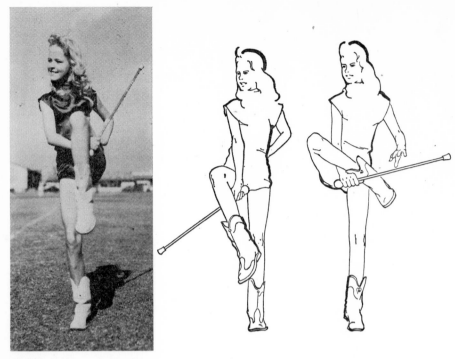

23. Leg Wrap Around. Steps 6, 8, and 10.

8) Kick the right leg to the back as high as possible, remembering not to lean forward.

9) Return to starting position.

Repeat several times with each leg. You should move from the waist down only, the upper part of your body staying straight and still. As you practice daily you will find the kicks get higher, your body assumes the proper posture, and style and grace follow naturally.

LEG WRAP AROUND

The first leg trick is the Leg Wrap Around (Figure 23) which sounds complicated but actually is quite simple. Refer to the illustrations and take each step slowly to begin with.

1) Start with an Extended Arm Stationary.

2) With a downward wrist motion bring the tip of the baton to the front, holding the baton near the ball. Execute one exaggerated Figure Eight with the long shaft.

3) Raise the left leg, toe down, and push the entire shaft under the leg.

4) The right hand, holding the baton near the ball, is placed under the raised knee, palm down. The shaft extends horizontally under the left leg, pointing to the left.

5) The left hand is on the hip and the body leans slightly forward from the waist. The baton is raised to a diagonal position, pointing upward.

6) In this position, make two forward circles with the baton.

7) As the left leg is lowered to the ground, the baton is switched behind the right leg, palm turning up as the baton resumes a horizontal position, tip pointing back.

8) Raise the right leg to proper position, and roll palm down and to the right.

9) The right elbow pushes under the raised right knee, switching baton to horizontal position, tip pointing right.

10) A palm-down wrist motion places the baton, tip leading, horizontally in front of right ankle which has been crossed in front of left thigh.

11) Take the baton from Step 10 with the left hand, palm down, the thumb to the ball.

12) Dip the ball back behind the body at waist height.

13) Take the shaft with the right hand behind the body with thumb to ball.

14) Bring the shaft out with the right hand and start a Flat as you lunge forward on the right foot.

15) Execute two or more Flats, depending on wrist agility.

16) Conclude in a Waist Pose.

This is usually done to a count of 12:

Step 2 receives the 1–2 count.

Steps 3–4–5–6 receive the 3–4 count.

Steps 7–8–9–10 receive the 5–6 count.

Steps 11–12 receive the 7–8 count.

Steps 13–14–15 receive the 9–10–11 count.

Step 16 receives the 12 count.

This will give you an idea of the speed needed to execute the twirl once you have perfected it. The illustrations will answer your questions of body placement.

24. Leg Whip. Step 5.

LEG WHIP

When you have mastered the Leg Wrap Around you will find that the Leg Whip (Figure 24) gives little trouble.

1) Start the Leg Whip exactly as you would the Leg Wrap Around and proceed through Step 6.

2) Step down quickly on the left leg, bringing the right leg up in position as you whip the shaft back of the raised right knee.

3) Quickly step down on the right foot and repeat procedure to the left.

4) Place the left hand behind the waist at the back, extending the hand to the right of the body, palm up. Note body stance in Figure 24.

5) With a backward flip of the right wrist under the left knee, thrust the baton over the raised left knee, tip leading, to the waiting left hand at back of waist.

6) Grasp the shaft with the extended left hand, thumb to

the ball. You are ready to repeat the Leg Whip or go into another twirl.

As you practice you will develop a small flip of the baton from the right to the left hand.

Surely by now you realize the importance exercising has played in limbering your body for this more difficult beginner twirling and leg work. And I'm sure it is not necessary for me to repeat that you must *never* neglect exercise, particularly as we proceed into more complex routines.

AROUND THE BODY REVERSE WITH
TURNS AND STEPS

A clever leg combination is next. This utilizes an Around the Body Reverse, and the variation is in body positions as you execute the twirl.

1) Start by doing one Figure Eight in the right hand.

2) As you dip the ball back, quickly turn the body halfway around to the right, legs slightly apart.

3) Push the baton, ball leading, behind through the legs. Body bends from the waist.

4) The left hand grasps the shaft, thumb to point, in front of the body, as you would do to complete your Around the Body Reverse.

5) Cross the left leg in front of the right closely as you do Step 4.

6) Raise high on the half-toe and finish turn to the right as the baton completes its out, back, dip, back, motion.

7) Execute beginning Figure Eight with right hand.

8) Push the tip under the raised right leg at knee height.

9) Proceed with Around the Body Reverse baton motion as right leg returns to the floor. Step left foot to the left and step right foot to a closed position next to left foot, moving toward left.

10) Repeat this with baton dipping under left leg, ball leading, and footwork to the right.

You are thinking: Figure Eight and dip and cross and turn, Figure Eight and dip and step right, step left, close right, Figure Eight and dip and step left, step right, close left. The baton motion is the Around the Body Reverse, a

25. Around the Body Reverse Lunge. Steps 2 and 4.

twirl you know thoroughly thus relieving your concentration on twirling and applying it to body and foot work. Be sure to keep in mind that you turn toward the right.

AROUND THE BODY REVERSE LUNGE

While we are studying the Around the Body Reverse, let's learn the Lunge Turn variation (Figure 25). This also is a simple change of body position and Presto! you have an altogether different-appearing twirl.

1) As you start the Figure Eight twirl, dip the baton to about knee height.

2) At the same time, jump forward on the right foot, extending the left leg high to the back in a locked position.

3) A jump on the right foot to the right turns your foot and body halfway around. You now have your back to the audience.

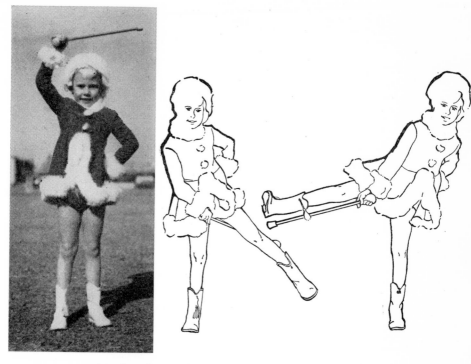

26. Leg Jump Over. Steps 3, 6, and 8.

4) The baton, dipped behind the right leg, is passed to the left hand which grasps it, thumb to the tip.

5) As the left hand brings the baton out from this position to finish the Around the Body Reverse, the body is raised, and the extended left leg is crossed in front of the right leg.

6) Raise high on the half-toe and complete turn to the right to face the audience.

Notice the body position in Figure 25. The left leg is extended straight and stiff.

LEG JUMP OVER

The Leg Jump Over (Figure 26) is not difficult. It is really restful, fun, and effective in group work. You may go into this from various twirls, but, for explanation purposes, let's try it from an Around the Body Reverse. Execute this twirl through the stage of passing the left hand back to the waist high position behind the body.

1) Grasp the shaft in back of the body, right hand close to the ball, thumb to the tip.

2) Extend the right arm and baton high above the head.

3) Rolling from a backward wrist palm-down motion to a forward wrist palm-up motion, make two circles over the head with the baton.

4) Palm down, the arm drops to the front left of the body, tip to the floor.

5) Raise the left leg straight out to the left side with locked knee and pointed toe.

6) The tip of the baton and half of the shaft make a half-circle to the back under the raised left leg and pass to the right.

7) As the left leg returns to the floor, the right leg is raised in the same manner.

8) The shaft of the baton is quickly passed under the raised right leg.

9) As the right leg returns to the floor, the right arm brings the baton high over the head in one more sweeping circle.

10) Finish with an Extended Arm Stationary Pose.

The legs must extend straight out at the side, and the body from the waist up is straight. Keep your head in proper position and don't drop your chin. As you practice, you will develop a quick jump from left to right as you change foot positions. This is sometimes called the Lasso because the overhead circle motion is similar to that used by the cowboy as he swings his lariat to lasso a frisky calf.

LEG CHANGE

The Leg Change (Figure 27) is a fascinating trick that requires more practice than skill. You will probably suffer bruised knees before this one is perfected, but the finished result is worth the pain. This is one trick where we can truthfully say, "Look, no hands!" It is much easier done with bare legs, so don't try it in tights or slacks.

1) Raise the right leg, toe pointing down and knee bent.

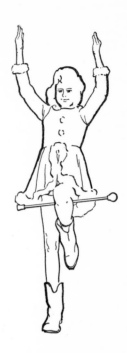

27. Leg Change. Steps 2 and 5.

Place the center of the shaft in the bend of the knee, ball to the right, tip pointing left.

2) Grasp the baton firmly with the calf and thigh muscles.

3) Place both hands over the head, palms turned inward, fingers straight.

4) As you step quickly down on the right foot, the left leg starts to raise, pushing 12 or 14 inches of the shaft forward which, in turn, pushes the ball to the left.

5) The tip end of the shaft rolls into position behind the left knee where it is grasped tightly by the calf and thigh muscles.

This is a good ending for a routine. However, if performed during a routine, grasp baton and go into next twirl.

It is evident that this takes quick foot work. As you practice, you will find that you actually jump down on the right leg as you are bringing the left leg up. When speed is developed, you will note that the shaft change actually makes its shift from back of the right knee to back of the left knee a second before the right foot touches the floor. It is impossible to practice this trick slowly. If you are not fast, the shaft will fall from behind the bent knee and roll down the leg. It requires a quick change from right to left with the muscles gripping tightly and the momentum of the baton swinging it into position. You must use force as you jump down on the right and raise the left leg. Until the Leg Change is mastered, the baton bumps and bruises the inner part of each knee in turn and sometimes flies gaily across the room as the leg comes up grasping nothing but air. This trick has tremendous audience appeal which makes worthwhile the necessary practice to perfect it.

TOE KICK

Another deceptive leg trick is the Toe Kick. The action is actually accomplished by the wrist, but we give the illusion that a kick has put the baton in motion.

1) Grasp the tip of the baton, thumb toward the ball.

2) Place the ball on the floor in front of the right foot.

3) As the toe of the right foot comes up to the ball in a kicking motion, the right wrist flicks the ball upward.

4) With a forceful up and back wrist motion, the shaft is flung into the air to spin a full circle.

5) The right arm is extended, palm up, to catch the falling baton, thumb to the ball.

As skill develops, the force behind the pitch increases, and the baton reaches a greater height, often making as many as three complete circles before it falls. The beginner is usually afraid of catching even the smallest pitch and is inclined to cringe or shy away. This is a natural tendency and is soon conquered. Keep pitches small at first and do them slowly. The motion of the baton will be so slow that there will be enough time for you to catch it easily. If you keep a palm-up position under the falling baton, it will drop gently into your waiting hand. Speed and height will be added as you gain confidence.

HITCH KICKS

Among the most striking kicks are Hitch Kicks which are more effective in stationary positions than with twirling motions. They are used mostly in parades and field work, but they also add interest to group stage work. Hitch Kicks require high leg motion and good body posture. They can be done either in place or while marching. Let's try them using the Horizontal Stationary.

1) Starting with left foot, do two Strut steps, left, right.

2) Kick the left leg high to the front, toe pointed.

3) As it starts to return to the floor, kick the right leg high to the front, toe pointed. Left leg is on the floor.

4) Return right leg to the floor.

5) Start Strut step again and repeat above.

Your mental count is: left, right, kicks, step. Both feet are off the floor simultaneously for a flick of a second, thus giving the "hitch." Try to land lightly after each kick! Majorette boots are heavy, and, on stage, loud thuds reverberate like the sound of baby elephants instead of saucy baton twirlers if you do not control your step. The last step on the right foot after the kick must be very quick. Actually, you cannot allow a full count for it. The count goes 1 (left foot Strut), 2 (right foot Strut), 3 (left leg Kick), 4 (right leg Kick, step). As kicks become higher and better coordinated, the speed of the foot work gives the illusion that you are suspended in space momentarily. This clever trick is well worth working on.

An interesting change from the Horizontal Stationary is the variation discussed in Chapter 4, page 59. The left, right, baton motion is done with the Strut and the up, up, with the kicks.

Hitch Kicks are helpful in resting the legs during long parades or routines, and they are ideal for the football field.

KNEE SWAYS WITH HAND ROLL

The basic Hand Roll is used in many leg tricks, and by now you should be performing it smoothly and deftly. Unless this is true, I advise you not to undertake leg work. This is obvious from the next trick we shall study (Figure 28).

28. Knee Sways with Hand Roll. Steps 2, 3, and 5.

1) Feet well apart, toes turned out, execute a Hand Roll in the right hand.

2) Keeping the left leg locked tightly, bend the right knee to the right and pass the shaft of the baton behind the bent knee to the left, thumb to the tip, ball leading. Bend the body to the right.

3) Grasp the shaft with the left hand, thumb to the tip, and thrust the baton out to the left.

4) Lock the right knee tightly as the left hand executes a Hand Roll.

5) Bend the left knee to the left and pass the shaft behind the bent knee to the right, ball leading, right leg tightly locked. Bend the body to the left.

6) Grasp the baton in the right hand and repeat Steps 1 through 6.

Compare your body stances with Figure 28. You will find that you develop a sway from side to side and, as the baton speed increases, you will note that the count becomes a quick 1–2, right, 3–4, left.

LEG ROLL OVER

Another trick which uses the Hand Roll is the Leg Roll Over. This calls for quick wrist action and lots of practice.

1) Execute one Hand Roll.

2) Raise left leg, knee bent, foot arched, and toe down, keeping right leg locked tightly.

3) The ball of the baton sweeps down toward the floor and is pushed by the right hand under the raised left knee and up over the top of the leg, ball revolving to point right, tip to point left.

4) Release the shaft with the right hand.

5) Quickly place the right hand, palm down, to the right of the left leg at same height.

6) Pass the shaft over the raised leg and over the right hand.

7) Finish with a "grab" Hand Roll motion, catching the baton with the right hand, thumb to tip, after it has passed *over* the right hand.

Hand placement must be quick for once you have released the shaft, the baton rolls with a great deal of speed over the leg.

HAND ROLL WITH NECK PUSH AROUND AND LEG RAISES

By combining the Hand Roll with Neck Push Around with a leg raise we have another effective leg trick.

1) Complete Hand Roll with Neck Push Around to the point where you have passed the shaft behind the neck as shown on Page 52.

2) Raise the right leg high, knee bent, foot arched, and toe down.

3) Push the left hand under the raised leg far to the right and lean forward slightly from the waist.

29. Chinese Split. Step 6.

4) Release the shaft with the right hand and let the baton fall to the waiting left hand.

5) Catch the baton, palm up, thumb to the tip, and bring it out from under the raised leg with a left Around the Body Reversed motion.

6) Right leg returns to floor as Step 5 is performed.

CHINESE SPLIT

Although usually classified as a Pose, I am including Chinese Splits (Figure 29) here because they require quick leg work to perfect.

1) Start basic Flat twirl in the right hand and quickly Cross-Turn.

2) Drop down on left knee.

3) Place right toe in front of left knee and slowly sink forward onto right knee.

4) Extend left leg straight back.

5) Weight of the body is on the right knee.

6) Upper part of the body is held very straight.

When doing Step 1, raise high on the half-toe as you turn. The Flat keeps the baton in motion. Do not use your left hand for balance as you sink forward on the right knee.

30. Split. Step 2.

Maintain Pose by leg balance. Keep left hand on hip or in posed position. To rise gracefully from the Chinese Split, first bring the left leg forward, bending the knee and placing the foot in front of the right knee, then raise body to standing position by pressing weight down on the left foot and right knee, without using hands.

SPLIT

Now is an excellent time to start practicing acrobatic Splits and Back Bends. These, added to twirling routines, are most effective and have great audience appeal.

1) Start by placing both feet together.

2) Simultaneously slide the right foot forward and the left foot backward and drop the body down as far as possible (Figure 30).

3) Keep erect as you drop down.

31. Back Bend.

32. Half Back Bend.

Don't twist the body. Face forward and slide down until you feel a pull in the thighs. It would be remarkable if you were able to achieve a full flat Split at this time. In the beginning, as with your first exercises, do not overdo for a strained muscle can be most painful. Splits are difficult but not impossible, and the time required to master them depends solely upon the amount of practice you devote to them. To recover from Splits, bring the left leg forward until you can place your weight on the left knee, slide the right foot back even with the left knee, and raise your body. No hands!

BACK BEND EXERCISE NO. 1

Both the full Back Bend and the Half Back Bend are used effectively in twirling. To prepare body muscles it is easier to start in reverse. Begin with a build-up from the floor.

1) From a prone position flat on your back with hands placed palm down on the floor over each shoulder, slowly raise the body in what is called "building the bridge."

2) The head is tilted back and down, and the back arches the body.

3) The entire weight is distributed between feet and hands.

4) Hold position briefly and then slowly lower to original position.

The high, arched back will develop as muscles strengthen.

BACK BEND EXERCISE NO. 2

Once coordination has developed the next step is to "walk" down a wall with your hands.

1) With your back to the wall, stand about 12" from the wall, feet well apart.

2) Tilt your head back and place your palms against the wall on each side of your head.

3) "Walk" your hands down toward the floor, arching your body away from the wall and keeping your head dropped back.

4) When the hands reach the floor, first the right and then the left is placed on the floor.

5) The body weight is distributed between hands and feet.

6) Repeat in reverse, "walking" hands slowly up the wall to reach original position.

This should be practiced until you find you depend very little on the wall for balance.

BACK BEND AND HALF BACK BEND

When you have achieved a sense of confidence, try the Back Bend by standing in the center of the floor and bending over backwards until your weight is held by your hands and feet. Rest in this position for a second and then, with a push of your hands, slowly raise your body to standing position. Practice this until you can gracefully and quickly drop into an arched Back Bend and return with ease to an erect position. For beginners, a cushion in back lends courage. To utilize the Back Bend in baton work, it is necessary to develop the ability to hold the weight on two feet and one hand while twirling with the free hand. Try this at first without the baton. Slowly sink into the Back Bend, supporting the body with one hand and both feet (Figure 31). The left hand is usually used for support. Here again practice is required, but if these instructions are followed carefully, there should be no difficulty. For your first Back Bend and twirl, try Flats. In this twirl, arm position helps balance the body.

The Half Back Bend (Figure 32) describes itself. The hands do not touch the floor. The left hand is on the hip, the head bends back to near waist height, and the right hand executes a Flat, first far to the right, then in the center, next to the left, and then back to the right. The arm is actually making a high circle over the arched-back body. Twirling with the body in this position is very difficult and will take lots of hard work to master. Its effectiveness makes it worth conquering.

Acrobatics are not appealing to all baton students for various reasons. Some may be a bit lazy and begrudge the time and effort needed to achieve perfection in performance. Others suffer a natural fear which makes muscles tighten instead of relaxing. Both laziness and fear can and will be overcome by determined twirlers who want to possess top-notch skill and proficiency and who are determined to become versatile and all-around performers. The more twirls, leg work, acrobatics, and body movements you have mastered, the better your chances are for being chosen for the Great Parade, the Special Performance, or to become the winner of a coveted trophy in the big competitions.

The routine set forth below includes many of the basics, leg work, and Poses. Since it calls for quick motions with wrists and body, you will have to spend much time practicing it. Please note that in places the count changes from a 1-2-3-4-5-6-7-8 to a 1-2-3-4. This calls for real concentration and agility. When you have mastered it, you may really feel a sense of progress in baton twirling. The routine is set to the always popular "76 Trombones." There are 50 counts of eight after the drum roll, and you will notice that often two twirls or two different body motions are completed through the eight count.

1) On the drum roll, march into center stage position, with left, right, left, right, left, right, left, right, doing Horizontal Stationary with baton.

2) Two Toe Kicks, holding Pose on each 8-count. Do to two 8-counts.

3) One Leg Wrap Around. Do to one 8-count.

4) Lunge on right and do Flats. Do to one 8-count.

5) Return to Waist Pose. Hold for one 8-count.

6) Around the Body. Count of 1–2–3–4.

7) Around the Body Reverse. Count of 5–6–7–8.

8) Flats in right hand. Count of 1–2–3–4.

9) Continue Flats as you Cross-Turn and go into Chinese Split. Count of 5–6–7–8.

10) Hold Chinese Split and do Flats. Count of 1–2–3–4–5–6–7–8 and 1–2–3–4–5–6–7.

11) On 8th count, return to Waist Position, still holding Chinese Split.

12) One Hand Roll, and, as you start to get up from Chinese Split, do one small pitch, raising the body. Count of 1–2–3–4.

13) With body in standing position, catch pitch with left hand and dip ball behind the body. Count of 5–6–7–8.

14) Figure Eights under the legs starting with right. Do to three 8-counts.

15) Turn right side to audience and do Cartwheels. Do to two 8-counts. Face audience again.

16) Figure Eights and dip and cross and turn. Count of 1–2–3–4.

17) Figure Eights, under right leg, step, step, close. Count of 5–6–7–8.

18) Figure Eights, under left leg, step, step, close. Count of 1–2–3–4.

19) Figure Eights, dip and Cross-Turn. Count of 5–6–7–8.

20) Around the Body Lunge. Do to one 8-count.

21) Around the Body. Do to two 8-counts.

22) Around the Body Reverse. Count of 1–2–3–4–5–6–7.

23) Extended Arm Pose. Do on 8th count.

24) Leg Jump Over. Do to two 8-counts.

25) Pinwheels Up and Down. Do to two 8-counts.

26) Cross, half turn, back to audience, Half Back Bend, doing Flats high over body. Count of 1–2–3–4.

27) Continue Flats as you come up from Half Back Bend and finish Cross-Turning to right and facing audience. Count of 5–6–7–8.

28) Hand Roll with Push Behind at waist level. Do to two 8-counts.

29) Leg Whip. Do to one 8-count.

30) Cartwheel. Do to one 8-count.

31) Figure Eights, Right Hand to Left Hand. Do to two 8-counts.

32) Around the Body. Count of 1–2–3–4.

33) Around the Body Reverse. Count of 5–6–7–8.

34) Full Split, with baton doing Flats. Do to one 8-count.

35) Continue Flats, holding Split. Count of 1–2–3–4–5–6–7.

36) Waist Pose. Do on 8th count.

37) Slowly raise from Split, doing Pinwheels. Do to one 8-count.

38) Pinwheels in standing position. Count of 1–2–3–4–5–6–7.

39) Partial Extended Arm Pose. Do on 8th count.

40) Flats. Count of 1–2–3–4–5–6–7.

41) Waist Pose. Do on 8th count.

42) Repeat Steps 40 and 41.

43) While doing Flat twirls, quickly Cross-Turn to left, making complete turn and drop down on right knee. Do to one 8-count.

44) Cartwheels in kneeling position. Do to two 8-counts.

45) Pinwheels as you rise to standing position. Count of 1–2–3–4–5–6–7.

46) Extended Arm Pose. Do on 8th count.

47) Hand Roll. Count of 1–2–3–4.

48) Neck Push Around, bring out in front. Count of 5–6–7–8.

49) Repeat Steps 47 and 48.

50) Around the Body. Count of 1–2–3–4.

51) Around the Body Reverse. Count of 5–6–7–8.

52) Around the Body Lunge. Do to one 8-count.

53) Leg Wrap Around. Do to one 8-count.

54) Lunge on right knee and Flats. Count of 1–2–3–4–5–6–7.

55) Waist Pose. Do on 8th count.

You can now see that the combining of two-hand twirls, acrobatics, clever Posing plus a bit of imagination, equals a clever, fast-moving routine!

7

Signaling and Formations

As MENTIONED in a previous chapter, signaling is the responsibility of the leader or drum majorette. However, every twirler must know signaling and know it thoroughly so that she is able to take over in an emergency. Signaling must be snappy. It must be given properly because the entire group depends solely on signals for direction and guidance.

The leader's whistle and special baton are the only means of giving signals. There are no oral commands. The whistle, which has a clear sharp sound, alerts the marching unit. When it is blown, every eye is turned upon the leader to see what signal will be given. The leader must learn to sound the whistle when the left foot is ready to step in keeping with the drum cadence, and this alone takes a lot of practice.

To give you the broadest possible explanation of signaling, I shall explain it as though we were marching along a parade route. While the same principles apply to marching on a football field or in an auditorium, parades are much longer and we will thus include all kinds of signals.

The band and marching units are gathered in starting formation. Lines are straight, and spacing is well distributed. Whenever possible, twirlers are placed a baton length apart. Twirlers are standing At Ease (Figure 33), left hand on hip or dropped gracefully at the left side. The baton is in the right hand, held near the ball, thumb to the tip and the

33. At Ease.   34. Attention.

tip pointing toward the ground or back of the leg. Feet are apart. The drum majorette casts an approving glance at the formation and gives one short blast on the whistle. This is the signal to come to Attention (Figure 34). Quickly place the feet together and, with a backward flip of the wrist, bring the baton up under the right arm in Under Arm Stationary, ball in front, tip pointing back. Left hand is placed on the hip. You are standing tall and proud. The leader executes a quick Left Reverse, turning her back to the group, and gives the Forward March signal (Figure 35). This is one long and one short blast. On the long blow, the leader, holding her baton in her right hand close to the ball and pointing it high in the air, executes two forward circles. This is the *forward* part of the command. Then, on the short blast, the leader snappily points the tip of the baton to the front, with her right arm held stiff and diagonally away from her body. The drums roll, and, as each marcher steps out smartly on the left foot, the parade has started.

As the parade transits along the route, the next signal might be a Right Turn. This is similar to the Forward March signal. A single blast alerts the group, and the leader, baton in the right hand held near the ball, makes two circles and points the tip diagonally to the right. The group marches up to the place where the leader has signaled before turning right. In marching, all turns are made with a "squared off" step, stepping out in the new direction on the left foot after pivoting the body on the right foot. The whistle is blown as the right foot hits the ground, and you pivot, stepping out on the left foot. To make the right turn, the marcher pivots to the right and steps out on the left foot, to the right. The Left Turn signal is given in the same way except the baton is pointed to the left. The marcher pivots to the left on the right foot and steps out on the left foot.

Sometimes it is necessary for the leader to slow down the pace of the group if spacing becomes irregular. To do this, the leader reverses on the left foot and faces the group, baton high over the head in a horizontal position. The whistle is blown once, and immediately the marchers reduce the length of their steps. They do *not* slow down the rhythm for the drum beat stays the same. The leader marches backwards, maintaining the Slow Down signal until the formation has fallen into smaller-spaced steps. The leader continues to march backwards, facing the group, with baton held in Slow Down position, until it is possible to resume the regular pace. At that point, the leader reverses to the left, faces forward, and marches in the normal manner. The group resumes its standard marching stride.

The leader must always be conscious of the group behind her. Quick glances back and Turn Arounds are necessary, for at times the formation may become straggly or ragged. If the group stretches too far out of line, the leader may bring the entire formation to a halt and line it up, maintaining the beat. When this is necessary, the leader makes a Left Reverse and marches to the leading person in each line in turn. She gives a short whistle blast and holds the baton to

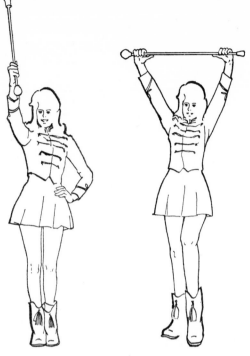

35. Signal to Forward March.   36. Signal to Halt.   37. Signal to Spread Out.

the front, horizontally, right arm extended away from the body, nose height. This signals the marchers to place themselves in line with the extended baton.

To halt the group, the leader reverses her position and faces the marchers, holding the baton high above her head in a horizontal position (Figure 36). She gives a quick blast on the whistle as she brings the baton down to a waist high position. There is a left, right, count after the Halt signal for which the mental count is: halt, one, two. All movement ceases, and the group stands at Attention.

The leader is always alert for what may lie ahead in the route. When leaving a wide street and approaching a narrower one, it is necessary to close ranks or bring the group closer together. This is done by the leader making the usual Left Reverse, facing the unit, blowing the whistle, and extending the baton to the front, horizontally, away from the body at nose height. The left arm is extended horizontally away from the body, fingers straight and palms turned inward toward the baton. The left arm is moved toward the shaft to a 1–2 count, held in this position for another 1–2 count, and moved back left with a 1–2 count. This Close Up signal is repeated until the ranks are closed. The marchers move closer together as well as forward while this Close Up is performed. There is, of course, a signal to open or spread out the ranks (Figure 37). The baton is held in the same manner, but the left arm moves away from the baton to a 1–2 count, is held in this "open" position for a 1–2 count, and these motions are repeated until the ranks are sufficiently open. Marchers move apart while continuing to stride forward to the music.

A Countermarch is showy, and it must be executed with precison to be effective. Signaling is not difficult, but keeping a straight line formation is. The signal is the same as the Forward March: two whistle blasts by the leader holding the baton high, tip front, and at right arm's length throughout the entire Countermarch. To Countermarch means to reverse marching direction. Each line moves up to the spot where the signal was given, executes a Left Reverse, and then marches back through the ranks of the formation. This is continued until the entire group has reversed its direction. Each marching line must execute the Left Reverse with precision and stay in an exact line as it marches abreast through the oncoming formation, keeping to its *own left* of the forward-marching lines. It sounds confusing and at first it can be, but practice, as said before, makes perfect. A Countermarch adds color to parade work and can be done when the formation has come to a halt. The leader must be certain, however, that there is enough time to execute two complete Countermarches. Chaos will result if there is not sufficient time and the parade starts again with your group marching in the wrong direction.

The best place for the Countermarch is the football field. Here as the unit reaches the goal posts, a Countermarch can be executed to bring the formation to the center of the field or to the other goal posts.

All baton signals must be performed high enough to enable those in the very back rows to see and understand them. Signals must be given with quick and confident motions, and the leader cannot seem to hesitate. The great responsibility resting on the leader is understandable. If a signal is given on the wrong foot, the entire unit is immediately out of step. If the leader does not close ranks when the group enters a confined area, the unit loses its smart formation. If the leader does not call for a slow-down, the marchers might approach dangerously close to a stalled float. The leader must be able to direct her group around such obstacles, execute quick halts when trouble develops, and, above all, give every signal clearly and at the proper time. When marching with a band, the leader signals the band to start playing: two short blasts of the whistle. Consideration must be shown the musicians so as not to exhaust their playing ability in the first few blocks of the parade.

A good leader is conscientious, considerate, and confident. The appearance of a marching unit depends upon its leader. Since there are no verbal commands, signals must be as clear as words. The actual placing of the baton is simple, but the perfect execution of signaling takes much practice.

There are numerous formations that marching units may make: letters, numbers, symbols. In Japan, one of our groups made the very intricate *torii* (gateway to a Shinto shrine), and, in England, during a rainy period, we formed an umbrella. What you can accomplish in formation work depends on the size of the unit. If the group is large or if it works with a band of some size, there is no end to the imaginative things that can be created. Small groups, however, must limit their efforts. Even the smallest unit can make a V, a square, or a circle. Clever variety in performances at football or basketball games adds interest to your formations. Since space in gymnasiums is usually limited, you must take this into consideration when planning your program. At basketball games the band usually stays on the bandstand, and only the twirlers present a show.

Plan your formations according to the size of the group. If a small unit, try V's or T's, or march in a circle or semicircle. A bit of imagination applied to your routines makes these simple formations very effective.

When you are marching with a band, the bandmaster will usually decide the formation placings. However, the occasion may arise when you must do the creative planning. First, determine *what* you wish to form and what position the marchers will be in when you complete the design. Number each member and think of these individuals as numbers while planning. It is wise to sketch your design on paper and move the numbers to the most logical positions. In actual practice, some changes may have to be made as the group works on the design, and the routine thus irons itself out. The following sketch gives you a rough idea of what steps you must take to achieve the design. The finer details will be polished up as the unit practices. As an example, here is a group of 36 marchers, two majorettes, and a leader in a formation I have often used. I have mentally placed the unit in the middle of a football field with the goal posts at either end. We have just finished a Countermarch and have proceeded to the 50-yard line area. We are facing one goal post, our backs to the other. The first sketch shows this position.

GOAL POST ↑

```
 1   2   3   4
 5   6   7   8
 9  10  11  12
13  14  15  16
17  18  19  20
21  22  23  24
25  26  27  28
29  30  31  32
33  34  35  36
37              38
        39
```

GOAL POST ↓

Leader and drum majorettes in front, the marching group has its back toward one set of goal posts and faces the other.

A Right Face signal turns us so that we are facing the cheering section, and the leader brings us to a Halt position. The letters we are to form are our school's initials, C.H.S. Numbers 37 and 38, the drum majorettes, will make the periods after the C and the H, while the leader will form the period after the S.

The leader gives the signal and the twirlers march smartly to previously assigned places. You will notice that some twirlers do not move. They stay in place and mark time. The letters must be formed quickly in the space of a few counts because it is important not to bore the *audience* by sluggish movements.

```
              GOAL POST ↑
   12  11            16              24
   8       7
   4                 15 –20–19–18–17– 23
   3                 14              22
   2       10
   1       9          13              21  38
     5   6   37
                 28  32  36
               27
                 31    35
                      34
                        33
                        30
             26  25  29        39
              GOAL POST ↓
```

We have formed the letters C., H., and S.

After holding the formation during the playing of the school song, the unit returns to marching position the same way it went into it. Then the leader gives the Left Face and Forward March signals, and the group marches off the field. Making the design, coming out of the design, and marching off the field must be practiced and polished to the point where they require only a few moments. Performance must be exact, movements trim and sharp. Even a few inches' deviation can disrupt a carefully worked-out design. It is each marcher's responsibility to know her part and to do it perfectly, and it is the leader's responsibility to take the unit swiftly and smoothly through its routine.

In some groups the leader carries the Signal Drum Major baton. This baton is not twirled but used only in Stationaries and signals. It usually has a white or walnut shaft and a colorful cord running down the shaft, ending in a small tassel at the beginning of the tip. It is longer than the standard baton, usually about 44″, and it weighs around 20 ounces. Because of its size and color it can be clearly seen by the smallest member in the back row. There was a time when this was the only baton used by the leader. In recent years though the drum majorette, who also wishes to do a bit of twirling along the route, has adopted the ordinary baton. The decision as to which baton is to be used depends upon the teacher, bandmaster, sponsor, or the group itself.

Although signaling is done only by the leader, it is important that every twirler learn how to perform signals. The day may never come when you would be responsible for signaling, but, by familiarizing yourself with the signals, you are able to anticipate and understand the leader, and, if the time should arrive when it is up to you to lead the unit, you are prepared!

8

More Difficult Twirls

NOW YOU have progressed to more difficult twirling in which both hand and body movements are used at the same time. By diligent practice of the previously described twirls and exercises you have developed coordination and body control. You may find that even though this chapter is devoted to more difficult twirls, you will perfect them much faster than you did the basics and their variations. The terminology is no longer strange. You have begun to "sense" the proper body stance, and the baton is an extension of your arms. You are leaving the novice stage and are ready to go into intermediate-beginner work.

REVERSED CARTWHEEL

A good start in this field is the Reversed Cartwheel which is almost a complete reverse of the basic Cartwheel.

1) Start by reversing the Pinwheel, using a *backward* wrist motion to bring the tip to the outside of the arm, ball under the arm.

2) The arm is raised from waist position to high above the head as you do Step 1.

3) In this extended arm position, execute a high Figure Eight.

4) Dip the ball to the back and down to the side into starting position again.

By using a backward wrist motion in Step 1, the baton, of course, turns toward the back.

38. Here-and-There. Steps 1 and 2.

HERE-AND-THERE

Another showy twirl combines the Forward Cartwheel and the Reversed Cartwheel with body action. We named this the Here-and-There, for the body turns from here to there on every fourth count (Figure 38).

1) With your right side to the audience, baton in right hand, execute one Reversed Cartwheel (Steps 1 and 2).

2) As the arm starts Step 3, a jump to the right shifts the weight from the left foot and turns the body so that the left side is to the audience. Baton is in the right hand away from the audience, and weight is on the right foot.

3) In this stance, execute a quick forward Cartwheel, as in Steps 1–5, on pages 44–45.

4) At the completion of this, a quick jump to the left puts the weight on the left foot, and once again you start the Reversed Cartwheel.

39. Flat Spin. Step 2.   40. Flat Pitch. Step 4.

Refer to the illustrations so that you can see correct body posture.

FLAT SPIN

Next we concentrate on more difficult Flat variations, begnining with the Flat Spin (Figure 39) and continuing with the Flat Pitch (Figure 40) and Flat Change.

1) Execute Flats in the right hand until the baton is spinning fast.

2) Quickly turn the palm up, keeping the arm stiff, and release the shaft of the baton.

3) The baton spins around your upturned palm.

4) At first the baton will probably make only two complete spin-arounds before it loses momentum. However, with practice, there is no limit to the number of turns it can make. If you feel it slipping, quickly grasp the shaft with thumb to the ball and go into Flats again.

FLAT PITCH

1) Extend your right arm to the side as you start spinning Flats.

2) With a strong upward wrist motion release the shaft.

3) The momentum of the baton makes it spin in its Flat position in the air.

4) Hold the right hand, palm up, under the falling shaft to catch it.

I suggest slow, low pitches in the beginning until you have perfected your catching ability, then add speed and height.

FLAT CHANGE

1) In this simple variation combining both hands and a pitch, start the Flat in right hand position.

2) Bring the right arm to center front of the body and release the shaft to the waiting left hand.

3) The left hand takes the shaft, thumb to the ball, and continues the Flat twirl without a pause in motion as it moves to the left side of the body.

4) The left hand releases the shaft and pitches it to the right hand.

5) The pitch is caught by the right hand, thumb to the ball, and the Flat twirl is continued smoothly.

This is done to an 8-count: 1–2–3 count is the Flat in the right hand with the change taking place on the 4th count. 5–6–7 count is the Flat in the left hand with the pitch to the right hand taking the 8th count. Your mental count is 1–2–3 (change) 5–6–7 (pitch-catch).

FLAT CHANGES WITH HIGH LEG KICKS

Combining leg work and Flats, here is a new twirl (Figure 41):

1) Execute the Flat in the right hand and push the baton under the right leg which is kicked high to the front.

2) Grasp the baton in the left hand, thumb to the ball, and go quickly into Flat twirls.

3) Return right leg to the floor and kick the left leg high in front and pass the baton under the left leg. Grasp it with the right hand, thumb to the ball.

41. Flat Change with High Leg Kick. Step 1.

42. Hand Roll Pitch and Ankle Catch. Step 3.

When perfected, this is spectacular in a marching routine. You step forward after each pass-under so as not to slow down the parade.

HAND ROLL PITCH AND ANKLE CATCH

As you have probably noticed, the basic Hand Roll appears often in twirling combinations. There are numerous body positions that may be used. Here are a few:

1) As the right hand executes a Hand Roll, the body is bent forward from the waist. The baton is pitched upward.

2) The right knee is bent, and the left leg is extended to the back in a locked position.

3) The left arm reaches under the bent knee (Figure 42)

and catches the shaft from the Hand Roll Pitch, palm up, thumb to the ball.

4) As the right knee starts to straighten, the body is raised to a standing position and the extended left leg is raised high off the ground. The baton, in the left hand, is brought out in the "out, back, front," Around the Body motion.

HAND ROLL PITCH AND WAIST CATCH

1) Do a basic Hand Roll in right hand and release the shaft in a pitch.

2) Place the left arm, waist high, far to the right in back of the body, palm up and facing away from the body.

3) With a quick body twist to the left, the shaft is caught by the left hand.

Don't turn the whole body to the left, merely twist the waist so you can place the left arm in a good catching position. The pitch is not a high pitch in this combination.

HAND ROLL HIGH PITCHES

1) Execute one Hand Roll in right hand.

2) With a forceful upward thrust release the shaft, spinning the baton high up in the air.

3) Catch in same hand, palm up.

You must practice Pitches (sometimes called Aerials) until you are able to guide their direction. Wild pitches are not only unattractive but can also be dangerous. In time you will achieve a high pitch without having to take a step forward or back to catch it. The shaft will sail high in the air, spin gracefully, and come down to catching position in the exact spot it was pitched. Much time and practice are required to perfect pitching and catching. Be sure you do not hold your palm stiffly for the impact of the baton can be painful. Your upturned hand should be relaxed but steady and strong. At first you will find catching as difficult as pitching because the shaft, as it falls, sometimes seems determined to avoid the outstretched palm, snubbing it completely and landing with a terrific bounce on the

43. Arm Roll. Step 2.

ground. Eventually, as your timing becomes coordinated, you and the baton will be meeting at the proper moment.

Body motion added to high Aerials is effective. When you have executed the Hand Roll and released the spinning shaft, cross the right leg close in front of the left leg, lock tightly, raise up on the half-toe, and do a quick full turn. Don't worry about the baton. It has made its ascent into the air and has just started its return by the time you have finished your turn-around. Stretch your hand out, palm up, and the shaft will fall neatly into it.

In teaching high Aerials to beginners, I find that if the right hand is used for pitching, it is much easier to catch with the left hand. Try this method in the beginning, but, as you become skilled, pitch and catch with either hand.

ARM ROLL

Rolls can be done with more than just the hands as the next three twirls will show (Figures 43–45).

1) As the right hand does one Hand Roll, the left arm is extended front and away from the body in a horizontal position.

2) The right hand catches the baton, and the ball is pushed down and across the body under the extended left arm. The shaft is raised up on the left side and over the the left arm, part of the shaft resting on the arm, ball pointing to the right.

3) The right arm is quickly passed from under the extended left arm to the right, ready to grasp the shaft, thumb to the tip as the baton rolls over the left arm.

4) You are in position to repeat the Arm Roll.

ELBOW ROLL

1) As one Hand Roll is done with the right hand, the left hand is brought up to the neck with the back of the hand resting on the left side of the neck, palm turned away from the neck, thumb toward the left cheek, and the bent elbow held high with the entire arm flat.

2) The ball is pushed down from the Hand Roll to the left and is brought up over the arm between elbow and wrist. It is released by the right hand.

3) The right arm is brought up in the same position as the left arm, above the extended ball.

4) The right elbow does a quick chop-down motion, hitting the shaft just below the ball with force enough to flip the tip from its left position to the right shoulder.

5) The left arm is quickly placed in catching position in back of the body at waist height, palm facing away, thumb up.

6) The baton slides over the right shoulder, down to the waiting left palm which grasps it, thumb to the tip.

7) The baton is brought to the front of the body.

If the arm is held in a flat high position during Step 2, the shaft will not roll off. This *is* a difficult trick and must

44. Elbow Roll. Steps 2, 3, 5, and 6.

45. Shoulder Roll. Steps 1, 4, and 6.

be finished in an 8-count: the Hand Roll is the 1–2 count, over the left elbow and the chopping motion is the 3–4 count, and the roll over the right shoulder is the 5–6 count. On the 7–8 count the baton is caught in back and brought to the front of the body. It is obvious that lots of speed must be developed to do this properly.

SHOULDER ROLL

1) The baton is held high overhead in a Horizontal Stationary, right hand near the ball and thumb to tip, left hand near the tip with thumb to ball, palms down.

2) Snap the baton down behind the head to shoulder level. The palms are now rolled into a backward position.

3) As you release the shaft with both hands, you must quickly (and it must be quickly) place the left hand in back of your body slightly above waist level.

4) The left hand grasps the falling baton near the tip, thumb to the ball, as it rolls down the back.

5) The left hand guides the baton down the back below the buttocks.

6) The right leg is kicked straight out to the side and the baton is pushed by the left hand from behind under the raised leg.

7) The right hand grasps the shaft from the front, thumb to the ball, and brings the baton out in any twirl desired.

8) During Step 7 the right leg is returned to the floor.

Although showy, the roll is not difficult, and you should be able to learn it without too much trouble. When it is perfected, the left hand motion is not even noticed. The baton seems to fall from the high horizontal position and roll down the back without guidance or help: a wonderful illusion and a unique bit of trick work.

BODY WRAP AROUND

On the other hand, the Body Wrap Around (Figure 46) is very difficult. This twirl describes itself. The baton is literally wrapped around the neck, the waist, and the legs. Again, time, patience, practice, and a limber, coordinated body are required. It must be done with the speed of light and the grace of a gazelle. Both the shoulder and hip pushes that are described go completely unnoticed in a finished performance when you have perfected your technique.

1) Do one Hand Roll, catching the baton very near the tip in the right hand.

2) Bring the arm up over the head and execute two complete circles as done in the Leg Jump Overs on page 80.

3) Push the baton to the back of the neck and complete the execution as was done in the Neck Push Around on page 52.

4) Release the shaft from the neck into the left hand which holds it close to the ball, thumb to the tip.

5) Raise the left arm high over the head and make two circles, this time however, with a backward wrist motion so the shaft swings toward the back.

46. Body Wrap Around. Steps 8 and 14.

6) Holding the baton by the ball, sweep the left arm down to the left side and dip the tip in back of the body, extending the left arm far to the right at waist level.

7) The tip and a sizable portion of the shaft are in a forward horizontal position at the right of the body while the left hand holds the ball.

8) The right arm is placed at waist level at the back of the body behind the left hand, palm extended as far to the left as possible.

9) A quick forward thrust of the left hand releases the shaft and starts the roll around the waist.

10) The shoulders turn slightly to the left and, to continue the shaft's roll, a sudden quick push with the hips to the left swings the baton around the waist into the waiting right palm where it is caught at the tip, thumb to the ball.

11) A sweeping right arm motion brings the shaft out from back waist-high position.

12) The ball points to the floor as the right arm brings the shaft across the front and to the far left of the body.

13) As the knees bend, the baton is passed behind the legs at knee level, ball leading. The right hand holds the shaft at the tip, thumb to the ball, palm turned out and wrist rolled forward. The body is in a squatting position.

14) The left arm moves across in front of the bent knees and grasps the shaft near the right knee, palm down, thumb to the ball.

15) The right hand releases to the left hand.

16) As the body is raised to standing position, the left hand executes a Figure Eight, dips the ball in back to the right where the right hand takes the shaft, thumb to the ball, in position for another twirl or a Pose.

HURDLE JUMP

This twirl uses a Figure Eight and an Around the Body Reverse motion.

1) Start with one Figure Eight in the right hand.

2) Dip the ball down and at the same time jump high, knees bent and close together. The baton is passed from right to left under the knees while the body is in the air.

3) The left hand grasps the shaft, thumb to the tip, as it completes its pass under the knees, and finishes with an "out, back, and dip, back," Around the Body Reverse motion.

Practice is needed to produce the high jump that adds decided style to your appearance.

OPEN LEG JUMP

Here is another jump (Figure 47) that utilizes almost the same motion.

1) Legs slightly apart, do one Figure Eight with the right hand.

2) On the second dip, push the baton behind the body and dip the ball between the legs.

3) Simultaneously, jump high into the air while the left hand takes the baton, thumb to the tip.

47. Open Leg Jump. Step 3.

4) The left hand grasps the baton as the jump is completed, and the motions of Step 3 finish the twirl.

Study Figure 47 for proper body stance and note carefully how the left hand is in position to grasp the baton while the body is in the air.

WAIST PULL

1) Execute a Lunge, ball on the floor, right leg bent and left leg extended back in a locked position, the right hand holding the baton at the tip, thumb to the ball, arm extended.

2) The right arm pulls the shaft back and releases it around the body at waist level to the waiting left hand.

3) The left hand brings the baton to the front of the body.

48. Thumb Twirl. Steps 1 and 4.

SHOULDER PULL

The Shoulder Pull is almost the same as the Waist Pull, but it requires a stronger thrust to raise the baton higher.

1) Execute a Lunge, ball on the floor, right leg bent and left leg extended back in a locked position, the right hand holding the baton at the tip, thumb to the ball, arm extended.

2) The right arm pulls the shaft back and up with a forceful motion and releases the shaft.

3) The shaft passes up over the right shoulder.

4) It is caught in back by the left hand, palm turned away from the body, as it slides down the back from the right shoulder.

THUMB TWIRL

The Thumb Twirl (Figure 48) is a popular favorite, excellent for both parade and stage work, requiring both hands.

1) The baton is held in the right hand, thumb to the ball, palm down, at waist level. Ball is to the left, tip to the right.

2) The wrist rolls back to the right until the ball has made a complete circle. This calls for a limber wrist.

3) The shaft, near the tip, has now rolled over the top of the right wrist.

4) The left hand takes the baton, near the right wrist, palm up, between the thumb and first finger, thumb away from the body and pointing to the tip. The right hand releases to the left hand.

5) The left hand rolls to a palm down position, thus moving the tip from right, to left, to right.

6) The baton is now in a horizontal position at waist height in front of the body.

7) The right hand grasps the shaft, thumb to the ball, and repeats Steps 1 through 7.

Be sure to grasp the baton in the middle of the shaft. Don't let your hands come too close to the ball or the tip, because this will throw you off the rhythm you are developing, the shaft spinning being out of proportion. One way to develop technique for the Thumb Twirl is to use an Around the Body break. Do four complete Thumb Twirls and one Around the Body, and repeat several times. It is important to develop a good Thumb Twirl because in routines it and its variations are much in demand.

The more difficult twirls covered in this chapter should be reviewed diligently. Body placement along with grace and confident timing is the secret of smooth twirling.

9

Group Work Twirling

SOLO BATON work is appealing, but group work is fascinating. Nothing is quite as eye-catching as a smartly uniformed baton group stepping and twirling with precision, whether on the stage or on a football field. Pert and saucy Poses, snappy Stationaries, and high Aerial Exchanges are especially impressive. The things that can be done with a group are unlimited, but clever design of the routines is most important. Remember that in group work you must avoid repetition or the appearance of repetition. Other thoughts to keep in mind are to make twirl changes quickly and never do one twirl too long. A fast change from one execution to another, even though it is just a simple basic, adds that 'difficult' look to your performance.

UNWIND

The Unwind (Figure 49) is a particularly clever trick and fits nicely in any part of a routine. It can serve as an unusual opening, or be done in the middle to a drum roll, or make a most unique finale.

1) Hold the baton in the right hand in an extended Arm Stationary, thumb and first finger toward the ball, palm down.

2) Raise the left hand from the hip up to under the right armpit, thumb and first finger pointing to the ball, and take the shaft at the tip.

3) Pull the tip forward. As you do this, the right wrist rolls

49. Unwind. Steps 2, 3, 4, 5, and 8.

to a palm down position, the elbow extended slightly to the right. As the left hand pulls the tip forward, the right thumb position is changed from pointing to the ball to pointing to the tip.

4) The left hand pulls the tip to the left, bringing the shaft to a horizontal position over the head, and the right thumb is pointing to the tip, the left thumb to the ball.

5) From the horizontal position, bring the baton to the left into a snappy Salute Pose.

6) The left leg is dropped from Salute Pose to a bent knee position.

7) The right foot is extended to the right in a locked position.

8) The baton is moved to the far right with the tip at waist height.

This twirl is done with a quick 4-count. Steps 1, 2, 3, and 4 take the 1-2 count, Step 5 takes the 3 count, and Steps 6, 7, and 8 finish with the 4 count.

50. Knee Flat Pose.

KNEE FLAT POSE

A really cute combination for group work twirling is the Knee Pose Flat (Figure 50), which is the basic Flat, but body position adds style.

1) Start Flats in the right hand.

2) Keep a stiff, locked right leg and bring the left leg up and place it on the right knee.

3) In the pose of "The Thinker," place the left elbow on the left knee, making the hand into a fist and resting the chin on the fist.

4) The right hand keeps the baton spinning in Flats.

5) A look of boredom, a flirtatious smile, or an expression of weariness will add to the effect of this Pose.

ENTRANCE PITCH

Your entrance and opening business on stage must have audience appeal. You must enter with zip and action to catch the interest of the crowd or the attention of the judges. There are many clever entrances, and high on the list are Pitches. One of the most impressive is a high Aerial Pitch before the group has marched onstage. "Impossible!" you say. "How can we pitch before we've made an entrance?" Here's how:

1) One twirler is placed behind the curtains on each side of the stage.

2) As the drum rolls or the introduction begins, both do a Hand Roll. The girl on stage right must execute her Hand Roll with the left hand, and the girl on stage left does hers with the right hand.

3) Catch the Hand Roll near the tip, thumb to the tip, palm down, and swing the ball down toward the floor and then up high, releasing the shaft with a powerful arm motion.

4) The baton will spin delightfully across the stage.

5) The twirlers pitch in unison, and each catches the falling baton with palm up, near the waist.

Be sure the pitch is high and slow. By the time it reaches the opposite side of the stage it will have lost some of its altitude, and the catch is easily made. It is smart for one twirler to direct her pitch a little to the front of the stage while the other aims her pitch straight across. If this is not done, you might see two batons clashing furiously in mid-air in the center of the stage.

This Entrance Pitch takes only an 8-count, the usual count for an introduction. The audience is always impressed as they watch two batons, seemingly from nowhere, spin across the expansive stage. Immediately after the pitch, the rest of the group should march in so there is no lull in the continuity of the routine. This pitch takes time to perfect, but in every unit there are always some who excel when it comes to high Aerials.

Marching in under an arch is another effective entrance. Two members enter from each side of the stage and, strutting high, they meet in the center. With a quick forward motion of their right wrists they make two circles with the batons and extend their right arms high above their heads, to form an angle with the batons. The rest of the marching group strut in under this arch and take their stage positions. When all members are in position, the two who formed the arch may march either to the front or stay in the center, whichever spot is more effective for the planned routine.

A group can also march on stage in a single file to the first 16 counts in a straight line, take stage positions, then execute an Unwind to a count of 1–2–3–4, and finish with a Flat in a Waist Pose on the 5–6–7–8.

It is difficult to keep a straight line formation onstage in group work. Room is needed so arm work can be free and unconfined. Better results are achieved if routines are planned in a V formation, a semicircle, or staggered lines.

Once you have made your entrance, your routine must be designed to keep a smart pace with lots of style. Precision Posing is very good, but the Pose is held for only one count, usually the 4th count or the 8th count. Utilize Lunges and quick Cross-Turns. Done with precision, these have a spectacular effect. It takes a great deal of practice before each member is Lunging, crossing, and turning with split-second timing, but the results are so effective that they are well worth all your combined efforts.

Individual variations add sparkle and life to group routines. An example of this is the use of acrobatics. Let's take a group of seven twirlers placed in a semicircle with the leader in front. The first girls at the right and left ends sink quickly into Splits. The next two girls, one on the right, the other on the left, go quickly into Back Bends, while the last two execute a Cross-Half-Turn and dip into Half Backbends. The leader does the Leg Wrap Around, Leg Whip, or Hurdle Jump. All this is executed in unison and to a quick 8-count. The girls in the semicircle might be twirling Flats to keep a smooth continuity while performing the various body motions. You will create many individual variations as you become familiar with designing routines.

If your group is blessed with an outstanding twirler, feature her. As an example, the group might take a kneeling position, Extended Arm Stationary, or the Knee Flat Pose while the star performer goes through her paces. An unusual and appealing way to go into Kneeling Pose is to go down individually with each performer having one count to take this pose. Imagine that the Xs below are a twirling unit of nine:

X (leader)

X (1)   X (2)   X (3)   X (4)

X (5)   X (6)   X (7)   X (8)

You will notice that each twirler in the staggered two-line formation is placed so that she may be seen by the audience. At the planned music break or at a signal from the leader, No. 1 goes quickly into kneeling position on the 1-count. On the 2-count, No. 2 immediately takes the same position, and this is repeated through the 8-count until the entire group is in the same kneeling position. The leader takes the next 1-count, and the whole unit executes a twirl through the 2–3–4–5–6–7 counts, rising quickly in a Pose on the 8-count. Quick motion, perfect balance, and precision twirling are needed to make this effective.

Exchanging Aerials in unison always evokes applause from

the audience and makes judges sit up and take notice. This calls for many hours of practice because timing and coordination must be perfect. In this explanatory example, a group of five is used. Four members of the unit have marched onstage and proceeded through a small portion of the routine. At a planned music break, the twirlers take Pose positions as the fifth member marches on, twirling two batons. She uses four 8-counts: one to get onstage, two to exhibit some catchy baton work, and the last 8-count to march back to the four girls who have come out of their Pose to form a straight line, with their right sides to the audience. The girl with two batons proceeds into place as first member, stage left, of the line. All are doing Flats with their right hands, including the girl with two batons who holds her left baton motionless and out of sight of the audience. On the 1–2-count, the Flats are done, on the 3-count all pitch their batons to the girl behind. The pitch should be at medium height, spinning slowly, so only a little power is used in the wrist motion. On the 4-count each member catches the pitch. The last girl in line, having no one behind her, on the 3-count switches her baton quickly to her left hand, and catches the pitch in her right hand. She now has the two batons. The girl in first place, immediately after the pitch, passes her baton from her left to her right hand, and continues with Flats. In the beginning it is wise to allow a full eight count for this much of the routine because there may be drops, and catches may take longer than 1-count. As speed and proficiency develop, you can change to a quicker count. Repeat the routine in reverse: the baton being pitched to the member in front. At the completion, the girl at the head of the line again has two batons, and the unit is still performing Flats. When perfected, this entire routine will be performed to an 8-count: 1–2 Flats, 3 is the pitch to the girl behind, 4 the catch, 5–6 Flats, 7 the pitch forward, 8 the catch, and perhaps a Pose if this finishes the act. If the unit is going into another twirl, however, the extra baton may be placed on the floor until the number is finished. Any group will have a real feeling of accomplishment when this routine is performed perfectly.

51. Seesaw. Steps 3 and 7.

SEESAW

An interesting combination, originated by one of our groups, is the Seesaw (Figure 51). This is partner work and can be used to advantage in group work. Taking a unit of six girls as an illustration, the girls are placed back to back as partners, making three couples. Each girl on the left is No. 1, and each girl on the right is No. 2:

XX	XX	XX
1–2	1–2	1–2

1) All excute a Hand Roll.

2) The No. 1's do a Thumb Twirl while the No. 2's squat.

3) The No. 2's pass their baton shafts back, ball leading, around the legs of the No. 1's.

4) The No. 2's take the shaft in the left hand, thumb to the tip, and bring the baton out with an out, back, front, Around the Body motion.

5) The No. 2's grasp the baton in the right hand, thumb to the ball, and start doing a Thumb Twirl as they rise to a standing position.

6) The No. 1's have been doing Thumb Twirls during the entire routine.

7) The No. 1's now execute a quick Hand Roll, and Steps 1 through 7 are repeated with the partners reversing roles.

We developed this into a clever combination by executing the Seesaw twice. Then, when all are again in standing position, they next sink into a squat, doing Thumb Twirls, proceed into Cross-Turn foot work, and rise while turning. The group will all be turning *in*, which means that No. 1 brings the right foot front in the Cross-Turn and No. 2 the left foot. The body is raised to full height while doing the Cross-Turn, and all are again facing the audience. For our finale, we execute a Pitch, lunging forward on the right foot for the catch.

Music for routines does not have to be limited to marches. Jazz, Dixieland, even percussion sounds, can be used. One of my groups walked off with many prizes for a routine that utilized the Spanish rhythms of "Mamma Inez." For variety, we even added a few samba steps. When the cha-cha-cha was popular, we designed a parade routine to this tempo. Remember: originality is always appreciated and wins applause and recognition.

A final note on group work (and equally applicable to solo performances): happy smiles throughout the routine are a big factor in audience appeal and acceptance. The audience senses your feelings, and if you are tense, depressed, or ill at ease, this reaches the crowd. There is absolutely no reason for not smiling! You have confidence, you are exhibiting an art, and you have become skillful in this art. Pride in your performance and your proven ability to entertain and amuse should produce radiant faces. With a winning smile you let the audience or judges know that you enjoy performing for them and you appreciate their interest and enthusiasm.

10

Different Types of Batons

WHEN you have mastered the standard baton to the point of easy, graceful twirling, when your wrists and body are coordinated and flexible, and when you can perform leg tricks with lightning speed, you will want to expand your talents. You will want to learn how to handle various other kinds of batons.

Novelty baton work should be kept as a *novelty* and not as your trademark. Since it is unusual and should not be overdone, use it only to add an occasional bit of spice to routines and performances. If employed too much, its newness quickly wears off, and you may soon be labeled "the group that twirls lighted batons," or "the unit that uses hoop batons." If you have appeared several times before the same audience, however, you might then add a novelty baton routine to your next appearance. A lighted baton number at a night football game or at basketball half-time is a refreshing change, and the outdoor fire baton is also spectacular if not viewed too often.

Described below are the various types of batons available and some applications of their use.

THE RIBBON BATON

The ribbon baton (Figure 52) is pretty and not expensive. It consists of a well-balanced shaft and two tips to which are fastened different colored ribbons about 18″ long. These are secured tightly in the tips by metal reinforcements. Colors

52. The Ribbon Baton.   53. The Lighted Baton.

may be of your choosing: school colors, sponsor's colors, or any combination you want. The baton is ordered by length and costs under $5.00.

A group routine is eye-catching with the bright-colored ribbons floating and swaying as the unit executes its twirls.

THE LIGHTED BATON

Lighted batons (Figure 53) are striking, but their use is limited. A completely blacked-out room or field is needed to achieve the desired effect. Among the several different styles there is one shaped exactly like the standard baton, but with a light in the ball and tip. It works on the flashlight principle: when the ball and tip are screwed tightly the light comes on. The most popular design is the long, thin shaft with unbreakable plastic combinations on both ends. These are about 6″ in length, are solid, and can be screwed into the shaft at each end. When the plastic ends are screwed on, both ends light up. Colors may be varied by inserting small discs of colored plastic at the tip of the flashlight. Combinations of colors may be used to good advantage. Another type of lighted baton is made with a very thin shaft which is much too narrow to contain a flashlight. In this kind, two batteries are inserted at each end. Color discs may be placed at the tips before screwing on the plastic or lucite ends, or they may be placed in the ends. Pull off the end, insert the disc, and push the end back into its rubber mold. Special care must be given to lighted batons. After each performance, the batteries should be removed. Batteries sometimes corrode or twirlers forget to turn off the lights thus cutting down the life span of the batteries. It is most important to be certain lighted batons are functioning before a performance. The stage will be dark and if any batteries quit, the effect of your routine is completely lost. It is wise to insert new batteries just before a program to insure a satisfactory performance.

Simple basics are used in lighted baton routines. The effect of brilliant, colorful light dancing around the stage in Figure Eights or Pinwheels Up and Down is amazing. Do not use Poses, Stationaries, or pauses. Keep the batons in constant motion and move freely around the stage. The audience cannot see you, your arms, or your body. Only the glowing lights from the baton ends are visible, and, if you move from front to back and from side to side while executing the twirls, the overall effect is as exciting as a Fourth of July spectacle.

Before planning lighted baton routines for inclusion in a program, be sure the place where you are performing can be dimmed sufficiently, if not completely blacked-out. The entire effect is lost if the vivid colored lights are not visible. Always practice in a blacked-out area so that you may be sure the twirls are effective. Cartwheels, Reversed Cartwheels, Around the Body, and Flats are some of the twirls that have a totally different appearance with this baton.

Lighted batons, without batteries or flashlights, cost around $10.00. Some units buy only one and reserve it for

54. The Hoop Baton.

solo work. Sometimes members purchase their own, thus enabling more than one person to twirl a lighted baton in a performance. These batons are durable and will take much abuse for a long period of time.

THE HOOP BATON

The hoop baton (Figure 54) consists of a round, wooden hoop with a silver shaft running through the center, dividing the hoop in half. I find this baton very appealing in the hands of small children. Older children can, of course, use it too, but the sight of tiny tots spinning large hoops seems far more effective.

To add color to the hoop, run colorful adhesive tape around it. This can be done to match or contrast with costumes, and it gives a prettier, more finished appearance. Other decorations such as bells or glitter may also be used.

There is a limit to the twirls that can be done with this baton because the hoop interferes with movements. The Cartwheel, for example, would have no style at all. However, clever tricks may certainly be performed. Descending Thumb Twirls followed by jumping into half the hoop, raising the hoop quickly up over the body and repeating the Thumb Twirls is a good example. Finger Twirls and Three-Finger Spins, similar to Flats but using only the thumb, first, and second fingers, are other twirls well suited to the hoop baton. You will find as you work with it many more clever tricks you can adapt.

Hoop batons also cost about $10.00 and, again, a group may purchase only one for solo work.

TWO BATONS

Twirling two batons is a feat that obviously requires a lot of practiced skill and mind-over-body control. Many teachers believe that to achieve better and faster results, one baton should be thinner than the other. Others disagree and execute twirls with speed and perfection using identical shafts. Of course, the length should be the same. Start two-baton work with simple basics and work at them until the left hand moves as fast and is as flexible as the right. How far you can go from there depends entirely on the time spent practicing. Some examples of well-developed skill are: Forward Cartwheel with one hand, Reversed Cartwheel with the other, or a high pitch and catch by the right hand while the left hand does Pinwheels.

It is wise to know all types of twirling well and to excel in one field, whether it is novelty work, leg work, or acrobatics. When each member of a unit develops a specialty, the group will be outstanding.

THE FIRE BATON

Truly distinctive in its novelty is the fire baton (Figures 55–56). It makes possible a really spectacular form of twirling. Of course, as with any product that involves fire, there is a certain amount of danger. Just as one match can be destructive in the hands of a child, the fire baton can be

55. Metal Case and Fire Baton.

destructive in the hands of a performer who is unaware of the precautions that *must* be used, or one who has not had sufficient twirling background to use the fire baton.

The fire baton is a metal shaft of normal length, with thick black asbestos cloth wired securely to each end. The cloth is fastened in such a manner that it cannot come loose. The shaft is punctured with many holes near the ends, their purpose being to keep the baton cool for handling. (Although wooden shafts are available, I do not recommend them. They do not get hot, but they have a short life span). The asbestos tips are soaked in an ignitable fluid. This can be gasoline, kerosene, or a half-and-half combination of both. Gasoline burns brightly but evaporates quickly. Kerosene lasts longer but smokes and is difficult to light. The half-and-half mixture gives the best results. After the ends are soaked, they are lighted and the baton burns brightly at both ends.

56. Fire Baton Twirling.

When handled properly and intelligently, there is very little danger. In most schools there is a strictly enforced set of rules for handling fire batons. These rules *must* be followed by anyone using these batons. In my schools, a student never performs with fire unless I am present to prepare the batons, light them, hand them to the performer, put them out, and insist that every safety measure be followed. If you do not have a teacher, a responsible and safety-conscious person should always be present when you practice or perform. A fire extinguisher and first aid kit must be on hand. We have never had to use either of these items, but it is wise to be prepared for any emergency. The container for preparing the soaking mixture should be labelled GASOLINE and painted a bright red, which is the universal indication for combustible liquids. I soak the baton ends in advance, at home or when I am alone in the studio, and carry them, ready to use, to the performance. Some twirlers prepare their batons just before the program at the place where the performance is held. If this is done, be very careful that everyone present knows you are working with combustible liquids in order to prevent accidents. You will have to experiment with the length of time needed to soak the ends properly. It depends upon the mixture used and the length of the routine planned. In time, experience will teach you what proportion and how much time are required.

The fire baton should have a metal case (Figure 55) which is used for carrying, storing, and, most important, for extinguishing the flames. The case has a handle because it becomes quite hot after the flaming baton has been placed inside it. There is a pull-off top at one end, and it is a simple matter to put out the flames in the metal case. At the conclusion of a fire baton routine, the twirler passes the baton to an assistant who drops it in the opened case, jogs it in place, and puts on the tight-fitting top. The fire is immediately extinguished.

A very skilled twirler can put out the flames by a fast high Aerial. However, you will not master this for quite some time, and the metal case is the safest method as well as a most practical piece of equipment.

After the baton has been properly soaked, the handler should always wipe the shaft thoroughly with a clean cloth. Even though we soak the ends well in advance, clean the shafts carefully, and it is unlikely there would be any trace of the mixture still present, we take the extra precaution of wiping the shaft *again* before lighting it.

Proper costumes for fire baton work must also be used: no fringe, loose braid, puff sleeves, or dangling trim. The basic sleeveless leotard is most appropriate for a girl; a boy must be sure his slacks are cuffless, all braid and cording are secured, and sleeves are not full. Hair is another potential source of danger. It should be set close to the head if short, and long hair should be covered with a helmet or bathing cap. Skilled, advanced fire twirlers rarely use helmets, preferring to set the hair close and then to fireproof it. It is a simple matter to flameproof both costume and hair, and many teachers insist on this protection. An easy-to-prepare solution is made by dissolving nine ounces of borax and four ounces of boric acid in one gallon of hot water. Fill a sprayer with this mixture and spray both sides of the uniform fabric and also spray your hair. This is a recognized preparation, it will not stain, and it has no harmful effects on the hair or fabric. The spray treatment should be repeated prior to each performance.

Regulations on the use of fire indoors vary in all parts of the country. In many places, city ordinances forbid the use of fire inside a building unless a fire department representative is on hand. Some auditoriums completely forbid the use of fire batons. Be sure you know the rules and regulations of both the city and the auditorium before planning fire baton routines.

Although spectacular wherever it is used, I feel outdoor areas are the most desirable for fire baton work. Unlike lighted batons, completely dark areas are not necessary, for the fire glows even in the bright sunlight. Outdoor twirling does have some drawbacks but not as many as indoor performances. Common sense will tell you never to twirl fire in high winds. Remember too, if you are working on grass, it can be slippery. Judge your jumps and turns accordingly.

If you are twirling indoors, be sure to take into consideration stage curtains, props that may be stored in the wings, and the space allotted backstage for other performers on the same program. You will find that as soon as you light the baton, inquisitive people will rush to gather around you. This is a source of danger, and must be recognized as such. While batons are being lighted, someone must be assigned to control traffic and keep observers safely away. We have discovered that if a twirler holding an unlighted baton walks onstage to appropriate music or a drum roll, an assistant can follow and light the ends in view of the audience and thus eliminate confusion and possible danger.

A fire baton usually throws off a small fire spray for a few seconds in its beginning spin. Previously soaked batons do not do this as much as those soaked just prior to the performance. Regardless of when the baton was soaked, the handler should twirl the baton a few times and shake it *before* igniting it. This helps to reduce the amount of spray. Once lighted, the baton must go into immediate action. The first twirl should be two hands in front of the body to eliminate any spray crossing the body. The spray is momentary and disappears within seconds.

Fast twirling prevents burns. However, if you slow down there is a chance of burns. It is similar to running your finger through the flame of a cigarette lighter. If you do this quickly, your finger does not even feel warm. If you do it slowly, a burn results. In fire baton work, perform only those twirls you are most confident of. Because of the greater weight of the baton, it is wise to practice with it unlighted for several days before attempting to work with it lit. Never attempt to use the fire baton alone. A handler, whether a teacher or other helper, must be on hand to light the baton, pass it to you, take it back, and extinguish it.

I want to repeat that the handler (the person who dips, lights, and extinguishes the baton) should *not* be the twirler. There should always be two people concerned: the performer and the handler. The handler has no worries about routines or twirls. Her mind is free to remember every safety measure. In addition to the steps described before, she puts the soaking equipment back into its proper place, she pours excess mixture back into the container, seals it, and puts it at a safe distance from the lighting spot. She knows a combustible liquid is never poured on the ground nor in a wash basin drain. A single forgotten or overlooked precaution can produce disastrous results.

Fire baton, like other twirling, must be practiced diligently until confidence develops, and the very natural sense of fear is overcome. As you become acquainted with the baton and the safety rules, you will find it similar to standard twirling. However, you must *never* reach the stage of "advancement" where care and caution are not used!

There is, of course, a certain amount of drama associated with the fire baton. Capitalize on this! Music should be appropriate. The "Bullfighters' March," "Satan Takes a Holiday," and "Sabre Dance" are exciting background for fire twirling. High pitches are sensational as the flaming, whistling shaft floats in the air.

The advanced student soon conquers fire twirling and moves on to handling two fire batons. Here, sometimes, burns do occur, but the love of the unusual keeps the student determined to continue in spite of slight blisters.

The fire baton is also in the $10.00 price range, and the case costs around $5.00. The company from which you order your baton has available, for around $1.00, a pamphlet which contains much good advice on handling the particular type of fire baton you have chosen.

It must be remembered that when using the fire baton, it must be kept in constant motion or all effect is lost. Poses, Stationaries, or slow twirls should not be used. Body, Leg, and Neck Wrap Arounds and Shoulder Rolls bring the flame too close to the body and should be avoided. In addition, they are not showy enough.

11

Swiss Flag Swinging, Samoan Sword and Fire Knife Twirling

A BOOK on twirling would not be complete without some time and attention being given to the closely related arts of Swiss flag swinging and Samoan sword and fire knife twirling, the latter a recent development.

1. SWISS FLAG SWINGING

Group or solo work with Swiss flags onstage, on a football field, or even on parade, is a lovely and colorful sight. With wrists flexible from baton work, the basics of flag swinging can be learned quite readily. Flag swinging originated in the very heart of Switzerland, the birthplace of the present Confederation, where it has always been practiced by Alpine peasants during the summer months. Just when it originated, no one knows. Perhaps it was used years ago as a means of signaling over great distances. It is as traditional as Swiss yodeling. It is not a sport but a skill which is acquired through study, strength, concentration, and coordination.

The Swiss banner heads every parade of Alpine athletes, the standard-bearer marching in front of the procession with the Confederation flag of red and white. Occasionally the cantonal flags, of which there are twenty-five, are also used. As he marches, the standard-bearer pitches his flag high into the air, cheering as he catches it. He makes intricate figures in the air, taking special care that there is never a crease or

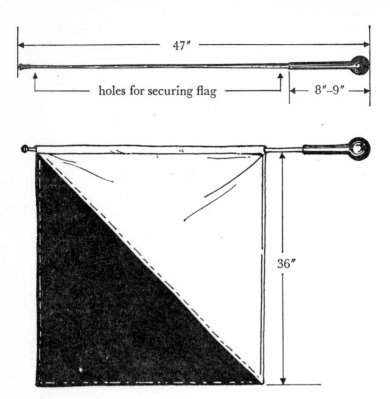

57. Flag Staff and Swiss Flag.

a fold to hide the white cross in its center, and never allowing the flag to touch the ground. The music is known as Oberland music, and the swinger's motions are keyed to it. The swinger at times uses one hand, then both hands, as he passes the flag between his legs, around and around his body, with a continuous smoothness.

This traditional skill has been passed from one generation to another, with children imitating their elders to learn the art of flag swinging. Championship competitions are held annually, and the experts, seemingly without effort, make the fluttering banners describe vertical and horizontal figures, execute high pitches, and perform clever leg tricks as they exhibit their skill.

My introduction to Swiss flag swinging took place in 1937

when my high school principal engaged an expert flag swinger to teach two other majorettes and me this skill. We were impressed by the intricate maneuvers and floating motions that could be achieved. The woodworking class made staffs with long handles, and the school colors of blue and gold in lovely shining satin were attached. We soon found our batons taking a rest while we developed some flag swinging techniques. In our area this was very new, and, needless to say, other schools were soon asking us to give them instruction. Flag swinging became so popular that we organized a group of several swingers to march with the school band. We learned that, as with baton twirling, improvising and adapting various twirls produced new effects. Many baton twirls, with a few changes, could be used with the flags. Soon we had an exciting collection of swings and throws that we could execute properly.

Although flag swinging has not grown in popularity as has baton twirling in the United States, it is used frequently and provides a nice variation in performance.

Flag staffs may be made or purchased. They are usually about 47″ long and $3\frac{1}{2}$″ in circumference (Figure 57). The handle is about 8″ or 9″ of the 47″ length. There are two holes in the staff, one at the top and the other about 9″ from the handle. Through these holes tapes or strong thread, attached to the flag fabric, are inserted and tied securely to keep the material from slipping on the staff. I have used staffs of all wood, wood and metal, and all metal. All have been homemade products and have served their purpose well. In one foreign country I could not find the long wood dowel pins needed in an all-wood staff. I substituted metal tubing $1\frac{1}{4}$″ in circumference and 37″ long. This was inserted and cemented into a ridged wooden handle 9″ long. Holes were pierced through the staff to secure the flag. This combination of wood and metal was most satisfactory.

The standard itself is usually about 36″ square after hemming (Figure 57). The fabric must not be too light nor too bulky. Satin is excellent. The material must be doubled so both sides are equally beautiful, and they may be the same color or contrasting colors. After hemming, the material is

58. Holding Position   59. Starting Position.

folded over along one side just a fraction of an inch wider
than the staff's circumference, and it is stitched down to make
an open-ended hem through which to push the staff. Because
the flag must fit snugly, it is important to have exact measurements before sewing. When the staff is inserted, the tapes or
threads which have been previously attached to the flag fabric
are pulled through the holes and tied. The material is
smoothed gently over the holes to hide them. Now that you
have a flag, let's learn some basics of Swiss flag swinging.

HOLDING POSITION

1) Pick up the staff from *underneath* the handle with the
right hand, palm up, thumb and fingers pointing away
from the banner.

2) Turn the palm in toward the body and bring the handle
in to near waist position (Figure 58).

3) About 1″ of the upper handle and about 2″ of the staff

rest on the arm, and the balance of the flag staff protrudes to the right.

4) Roll the wrist down and to the right to a palm-down position. This moves the flag in a circular motion, and it is now extended horizontally to the right of the body.

5) Raise the arm to shoulder height to the right, away from the body, elbow straight.

6) Palm is down, thumb points away from the banner. Bend the elbow, and you are in Starting Position (Figure 59).

You will find that the flag is much heavier than a baton, and its added length will take time to get used to. From Starting Position we will first try the Overhead Swing.

OVERHEAD SWING

1) The hand sweeps in front and then over the head with the wrist rolling to the far right, palm down.

2) The elbow is dropped to waist height, and the staff falls into the cradle of the wrist and elbow. Quickly bring the hand to waist position, and you are now in Holding Position as explained in Step 2 on page 142.

As speed and dexterity develop, the flag will stay in a horizontal position through the entire execution. At first you will find that because of your somewhat jerky motions the flag will curl about the staff, upset your hairdo, and take almost any position but horizontal. As you practice, smoothness and speed are acquired, and your beautiful flag starts behaving properly. To give you an idea of the speed, all these steps are done to a 4-count. The steps from Holding through Starting Position are the 1–2 count, and the steps for the Overhead are the 3–4 count. Concentrate on developing continuous, flowing arm motions.

Repeat with the left arm. You will note that baton practice has made the left hand more limber and far less awkward. However, if you have difficulty with the flag motions, remove the banner and practice with the staff only.

RIGHT TO LEFT OVERHEAD

When you are able to perform the above steps with speed and grace, by adding one more step we combine the Right and Left Hand Overhead, utilizing both hands. When perfected, this impressive swing flows in one smooth motion.

1) With the right hand perform the Starting swing, go into an Overhead Swing, and then back to Starting Position.

2) Sweep the arm to the left until it reaches the center of the body, wrist about nose height. The staff is now straight up and down.

3) The left hand grasps the handle above the right hand, palm turned away from the body, thumb pointing to the handle.

4) The left arm swings to the right, back over the head, the palm turns down, the wrist bends to the left, the elbow drops to waist level, and the flag staff falls into the cradle of the bent arm.

5) Using the left hand, go into Starting Position and follow Steps 4 and 5 of the Holding Position directions, remembering that you are working with the *left* hand.

6) Repeat Step 2 above (don't forget, left hand will sweep to the *right*.)

7) Repeat Step 3 above, this time grasping the handle with the right hand. Swing into Overhead with the right hand.

An interesting variation of this is to make your change from right to left with a small pitch. In releasing the staff after Step 2, force is used to give height to the pitch. Be sure to catch the pitch with your hand in the proper position, palm away from the body and thumb pointing away from the flag (Figure 60).

A perfect swing is a continuous movement without any pause. I suggest practicing these basics until they are mastered before attempting any further flag swinging.

As with baton twirling, you develop a "feel" in flag swinging. Soon your hands are grasping the handle automatically in correct position. When you have assimilated these basics, you will find you progress rapidly through the fundamentals of flag swinging. The basics are the foundation of many swings with only the addition of arm placements to create a different appearance.

60. Right to Left Overhead with Pitch.

Small pitches prepare you for the more difficult high pitches. With your right hand execute a Starting and an Overhead to the stage of passing. At this point execute a strong pitch, using force as you release the staff. You may pitch with the right hand and catch with the same hand, and then starting with the Overhead, repeat the procedure. This is also practiced and perfected with the left hand.

When you have become skilled with this part of swinging, put in several pitches before going into an Overhead: pitch and catch, pitch and catch, perhaps two or three times with the same hand before flowing in an Overhead.

From this basic we go on to High Pitches. These aerials are extremely difficult because of the strength required to toss the spinning staff and flag to a great height. Boys always do more spectacular flag pitching than girls. It is worth all the effort it takes because the sight of the flag and staff, spinning high into the air and floating down gracefully in a beautiful pattern to a perfect catch, is a very impressive one.

WAIST CIRCLE

1) Begin in Starting Position.

2) The right arm passes the staff to the back of the body, the arm holding an extended position.

3) The left hand grasps the handle, palm down, thumb away from the flag.

4) The left hand brings the staff to the front of the body and passes it to the right hand.

5) The right hand repeats, beginning with Step 2.

Speed keeps the flag completely flat, and hand action must be fast so that there is a continuous flow of motion.

LEG CIRCLE

An effective variation is the Leg Circle which takes a bit of practice to achieve smoothly.

1) From a Starting Position or a Waist Circle, with the right hand pass the staff horizontally behind the right leg, the left leg raised in a locked position in back of the body.

2) The left hand reaches behind the right leg and grasps the shaft.

3) The shaft is brought out under the raised leg to the front of the body by the left hand and passed to the right hand. Left foot is placed on the floor.

4) The right hand passes the staff behind the left leg while the right leg is raised in a locked position, and the above steps are repeated.

The body must be bent while performing the above. You will quickly realize that, as hand speed increases, fast footwork is necessary.

I suggest you practice this by executing two full Waist Circles, bending quickly, and, with the same hand-placing used in Waist Circles, continue with the Leg Circle through two full executions. Quickly rise to standing position and repeat two Waist Circles. Properly performed, the flag will stay flat and horizontal as it passes smoothly around the body and behind the legs.

Imagination and skill will help you improvise, and combinations of baton twirls will find their way into your flag swinging.

Since the flags are large, huge stages for group work are required. Such stages are rarely available, and group work is more or less confined to football fields or gymnasiums. Performances must be presented with precision to be effective.

In outdoor work, high winds will interfere with flag swinging. The wind will wrap the flowing banner around your body, completely destroy its horizontal flatness, playfully misguide your pitches, and sometimes blow the standard out of your hands. Postpone flag swinging on windy days, substitute a baton number, and wait for favorable weather.

To add novelty to a flag swinging routine at an indoor performance, fluorescent light and fluorescent material or paint may be used. Fluorescent light, known in the theatrical world as Blacklite or Stro Lite, is the light that, when a room is totally darkened, picks up the vivid colors of fluorescent paint or material. The flag might have designs or dots or lines in fluorescent paint on a darker background, or it could be made completely of fluorescent fabric. For best effects when using such materials, the performers should wear dark, solid-color costumes. When all illumination is blacked-out, fluorescent light works like magic—brilliant colors dance around the stage as you swing. Fluorescent lights are expensive to buy, but they can usually be rented from a theatrical supply house or dance studio. Since the performers cannot be seen, foot placing and body movement are of secondary importance. What impresses the audience is the gorgeous splash of color as the flags float through the air, and lots of action is necessary.

Fluorescent paint can be purchased at a theatrical supply house or a sign painter's, and both the spray can and jar are satisfactory. Materials can also be obtained from a theatrical supplier and they come in a large variety of colors and designs.

Floaty waltz music is most appropriate for flag swinging. Although hand and foot movements are done quickly, there is a lot of staff and a lot of flag, and they require more time to finish an execution than a baton does.

Considerable strength and concentration are needed in flag swinging, but a good swinger performs in an apparently effortless way with smoothness and a continuous, graceful motion.

When not in use, the flag may be removed from the staff by untying the threads inserted in the holes. It should be folded and stored in a plastic bag and it, along with the staff, should have a special storage place. There is no need to cover the staff, but it should be placed in an upright position. You may prefer not to remove the flag and may wrap it around the staff, covering it with a protective cloth. Don't hesitate to launder or clean the flag. In the beginning this will be necessary quite frequently.

Flag swinging, whether solo or group, adds another interesting variation to your list of expanding abilities.

2. SAMOAN SWORD AND FIRE KNIFE

Two unusual and interesting forms of novelty twirling have recently been seen in the baton world—Samoan sword spinning, which is derived from a famous Samoan dance, and the Samoan fire knife spinning, a similar technique, with fire added to the "weapon" for spectacular effects.

Samoan dancing, as is true of most primitive dancing, was originally a religious ritual dedicated, on that lovely Pacific island, to the gods of the elements: the sea and the wind, and to the goddess of the volcano. The sword, symbol of the warrior, was an important part of one of Samoa's most famous dances which was usually performed by two men. In this portrayal of a duel, one of the dancers conquers the other who suddenly disappears from the scene, leaving his sword.

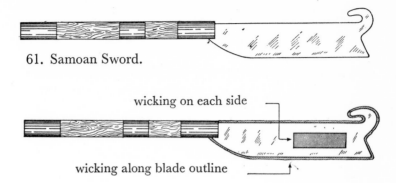

61. Samoan Sword.

wicking on each side

wicking along blade outline

62. Samoan Fire Knife. The wicking may be affixed either outling the blade or attached to each side of the blade.

The remaining dancer then hooks both swords together and finishes the dance with two flashing, twirling swords, a difficult feat requiring years of training. This was an art that was passed from father to son, and to be recognized for ability to perform the sword dance was a high honor.

These novel forms of twirling are so new that definite teaching formats have not as yet been developed by many instructors. I find the most effective way to twirl the sword or fire knife is to utilize Swiss flag motions combined with basic baton movements and various jumps.

There are two types of Samoan swords. One is made of spring steel (Figure 61), is about 30″ long, weighs around 2 lbs., and costs $30.00. The other kind is the same size, but is made of aluminum, weighs a bit over 1 lb., and is priced at $15.00. Both may be ordered from the Kraskin Baton Company, listed in the appendix. The sword handle which is about 16″ long is covered in wood with three metal overslips attached, the first one on the end, the second just a bit off center, the third near the blade. These overslips are for grasping during twirling routines. The blade, including the hook, is about 13½″ long and 2½″ wide, and it glitters and shines and gives an illusion of sharpness. Actually, the

63. Handling the
Samoan Sword.

64. Student learning the Neck Wrap Around
with the Fire Knife.

blade is very dull so there is no danger of injury while
learning and practicing sword spinning. As with all equipment, the life of the Samoan sword depends on the care it
is given. It is wise to provide a cover and specific storage
place for it when not in use.

The fire knife (Figure 62) is the dance sword with flame
added. The wicking may be affixed in the following ways:
(1) outlining the blade, (2) attached to each side of the blade,
or (3) attached to the blade and first overslip. The most
effective manner, I think, is to have the blade outlined by
wicking because more exciting and spectacular results can be
achieved. The fire knife costs around $35.00 and is available
at the supplier mentioned above. Special containers, similar
to the fire baton container, are a must and cost around $8.00.

As stated above, both flag and baton motions can be used

with the sword and fire knife, combining the two for the greatest effect. If the baton motion is used with the right hand, the left hand utilizes flag movements. This results in a more varied performance and permits more body movement, most essential in this form of twirling. Similar to modern jazz in the dance world, sword and fire knife choreography accents body motion much more than does standard twirling. There is real opportunity for individual expression, and, for the intermediate and advanced student, a most satisfying way to express personality and creative ability.

Coordination is needed before attempting sword and fire knife work. Start with slow movements until arms and wrists become accustomed to the additional weight (Figure 63). Listed below are practice exercises which must be mastered before studying twirls, which, combined with arresting body movements and appropriate music, produce striking routines.

Music other than marches is required. Percussion drums or bongos in Hawaiian and Polynesian rhythms add authenticity to the performance. Proper costumes are important. The military design that predominates in baton uniforms is not suitable. Bright colors typifying the south Pacific islands and styles that allow body freedom are needed to complete the picture. A basic leotard, gaily decorated in sparkling sequins, or a brilliant sarong might be used.

Samoan sword and fire knife spinning has not yet made its place in baton competitions, but, with the enthusiasm that is being shown, it is likely that in the near future it will be added to the novelty baton agenda. As you will note, the sword and fire knife present different problems in handling in that the manner of holding them varies with the twirl being performed. It is necessary to point out that the fire knife should be handled *only* by advanced twirlers who have had sufficient experience and practice with the fire baton *and* the Samoan sword. In addition, all the previously stated safety measures should be enforced when working with the fire knife.

Basic baton twirls—Figure Eights, Flats, Pinwheels— are considered basics for sword work. When doing Figure Eights and Flats, grasp the handle on the third overslip (nearest the blade), thumb toward the blade, palm down. This is grasp is also used for Around the Body movements Figure 64). Pinwheels, on the other hand, require you to grasp the handle *between* the second and third overslips, thumb *away* from the blade. This brings the handle and not the blade under the arm. When using flag motions, the handle is held by the first overslip in the same manner you would hold the flag staff.

Practice the basic baton twirls with both hands and practice the basic flag swings with both hands until you are accustomed to the weight, and then try some of the following.

OVERHEAD THRUST

1) Sword in the right hand, do one Overhead flag swing, holding the handle by the first overslip.
2) Lunge forward on the right foot, swinging the knife diagonally to the right.
3) Pose with the left leg extended to the left, toe pointed, weight on the right foot, and left arm posed gracefully in front of the body, waist high in a horizontal position.

LASSO JUMP

1) Execute one Leg Jump Over.
2) Finish with a Flag Overhead with the right hand and pitch the sword to the left hand.

HIGH WINDER

1) Start with Thumb Twirls at waist height.
2) Raise arms to position over the head, continuing Thumb Twirls in a palm-up position.
3) Switch to Shoulder Roll.
4) Finish with Lunge to left in a dance pose.

BREAKAWAY

1) Using the Flag Waist Circle, hold the sword on the second overslip, thumb away from the blade, palm down, and start the sword around the waist.
2) As it passes from right to left, bend the knees slightly

and jump, pushing the legs out to the sides in locked position.

3) Repeat twice.

4) Bend the body from the waist to continue circle motion and drop hands to calf.

5) Pass sword around the legs once and finish with high jump, bringing the sword above the head, held horizontally in both hands.

SHIFT

1) With the left hand do one Around the Body Reverse.

2) As the right hand passes back to the left, grasp the sword behind the body at the first overslip, thumb toward the blade.

3) Thrust the sword from behind over the left shoulder, blade down, to the waiting right hand which is held at chest level. This requires very agile left wrist motion.

4) Grasp the sword in the right hand at the second overslip and let the blade touch the floor as you lunge to the right.

HOOKSTER

1) Place the first finger of the right hand in the hook of the blade.

2) Swing into a Flag Overhead and then go into the Flag Starting Position, releasing the finger from the hook and giving an upward thrust of the right wrist.

3) Catch the pitched sword with the left hand by the handle.

HURDLE JUMPS WITH LEFT OVERHEAD

1) Execute a Hurdle Jump with sword in the right hand.

2) The left hand grasps the sword at the first overslip and goes into an Overhead flag swing.

DANDY

1) Do one Thumb Twirl.

2) Begin a second Thumb Twirl and, with the left hand, grasp the handle, thumb to the blade, palm up. Raise the arm over the head with a backward wrist motion.

3) Bring the knife back to the left and over the head.

4) Go quickly into a Reverse Around the Body, passing sword to the right hand in back of the body and bring out front in a Thumb Twirl.

LEG WIND

1) Execute one Figure Eight with the right hand, thumb to the blade, holding on the third overslip.

2) Raise the right leg, knee bent, toe pointed down.

3) Dip the blade behind and under the raised right leg and let the blade slide down the palm, catching it with the first finger by the hook.

4) Quickly flip the handle in front of the raised right foot. The handle and part of the blade touch the foot.

5) With the left hand reach under the raised right leg and grasp the handle on the third overslip, thumb to the blade.

6) Go into Figure Eight and repeat routine, this time with the left arm and leg.

SPIRAL

1) Sword in the right hand at the third overslip, thumb toward the blade, do four Flats.

2) On the fourth Flat let the blade slide downward, catching it with the first finger by the hook.

3) Go into an Overhead flag swing with the right hand.

4) As the handle swings to the front of the body in a vertical position, grasp with the left hand at the third overslip, thumb toward the blade.

5) Go into Flats and repeat from Step 3 with the left hand.

The above represent only a few of the interesting combinations of baton and flag movements which are effective with the sword. Having mastered these, your imagination will develop many more. Remember to intersperse them with showy dance poses which can be any of the standard ballet or modern dance poses. As has been said before, the more forms of twirling you master, the greater your chances for success!

Don't forget that certain twirls do not lend themselves to

the fire knife just as they are not suitable for the fire baton. Fast motion is effective, but momentary Poses, especially side Poses, may be used. Such twirls as the Overhead Thrust, the Lasso Jump, or the Breakaway are spectacular with the fire knife. It is important to remember you are handling flame and, as stated before, you should not attempt any twirls that bring the fire close to the body.

12

Uniforms, Footwear, Accessories

MANY things must be taken into consideration when choosing uniforms. As with everything else in this wonderful life, your first thought is of money. The amount of your budget is usually the deciding factor. It isn't necessary to spend a great deal of money to have showy uniforms. If you are working with a limited amount, inexpensive materials may be used. If you are less handicapped financially, better fabrics may be purchased. Both have their good points, and in this chapter we will discuss homemade as well as custom-tailored uniforms.

Consideration must be given to the climate in your area and also to the locale of the majority of your performances —indoors or outdoors. Most twirling units eventually acquire uniforms for both kinds of work. This can be done bit by bit so that the initial cash outlay is not necessarily great.

Another important decision is color. If you represent a school or organization that is identified by special colors, your uniform should be based on these. If you are free to choose, the colors selected should be flattering to all members of the group. Solid white with gold or silver trim is always an excellent choice, but, since it is widely used, you might want something more imaginative and unusual. Rich brown with bright yellow or gold is beautiful, as is green with silver, blue with gold, red with white. For inexpensive uniforms, theatrical materials with silver or gold metallic thread run-

65. Inexpensive indoor twirling costume with blouse, shorts, cape, bloomers, and skirt.

ning through the fabric are attractive. These may be purchased at theatrical supply houses and are no more expensive than ordinary satins. Uniforms should be designed with twirling in mind. They should be in good taste and, above all, well-fitted. Huge full sleeves, for example, are pretty to look at but are not practical for baton work.

Uniforms can be obtained in many ways. Often the sponsor picks up the tab for the entire unit. As I said before, a sponsor is a real asset. Some schools that want good, long-lasting outfits, purchase complete equipment and rent it to the twirler or marcher on a yearly basis. In other cases, the entire cost is borne by the individual. Before choosing your uniform, then, decide upon the amount of money you can afford to invest and make your plans accordingly.

Let's start first with the inexpensive indoor twirling costumes (Figure 65). These can be made of light-weight material with a sleeveless blouse that has a military collar, jacket zipper down the back, one or two frogs across the front with a strand of connecting braid. Plain shorts with elastic at the back of the legs (to assure a clinging fit) complete this

66. Princess-style costume with frogs, sash, and epaulettes.

basic outfit. Blousey bloomer tights are used only under skirts because they are too bulky to make a trim appearance. A strip of braid may be added to each side of the shorts.

For variety, a short cape may be added without much expense. The cape should not interfere with arm movement. This is done by cutting the cape so that it is attached at the shoulders with hooks and eyes. The cape may be lined with a contrasting color, and a 2″ fringe may be stitched around it. Fabric cost for blouse, shorts, and cape, using an inexpensive satin, would run around $3.50. Further variety in this costume is possible by adding a skirt. This may be pleated, circular, or gathered, and it will not cost more than $1.50 if you use the same kind of material. Thus, for under $6.00 you have a four-piece costume that can be worn in four different styles: blouse and shorts alone; blouse, shorts and cape; blouse, shorts, and skirt; or blouse, shorts, skirt, and cape. Be sure the blouse extends well below the waist to prevent exposure of bare midriff when arms are raised. Zippers in the blouse, skirt, and shorts are far more satisfactory than snaps, hooks, or grippers. The Jet-ettes used this kind of uniform in an inexpensive brown satin with gold trim. It gave good wear and a satisfying variety of changes for our numerous performances.

Another reasonable but elegant-looking costume is the princess-style dress (Figure 66) with a military collar and back zipper to below the waist. It is figure-flattering and works well for beginner groups. The skirt, which is a fraction of an inch longer than the tights, is lined from the waist down with rather stiff lining material. A striking color combination is white satin with three rows of gold braid connecting the frogs in front. Bloomer tights may be worn for they do not show and they do allow freedom. The long sleeve is slightly gathered at the shoulder and at the cuff, which is about an inch wide. On tall girls this uniform is especially attractive. For material only, this outfit also costs under $6.00. This uniform may be changed by removing the frogs and braid and attaching a bright red shoulder sash from the right shoulder across the chest to the left hip. It is tacked at the waist, and the ends of the ribbon are left free to hang to the hip.

A clever and different design can be produced by the use of stripes. For example, a cotton fabric with half-inch wide black and pink stripes, used vertically, forms the blouse which has a military collar, zipper in the back, and short full sleeves (Figure 67). A black circle or gathered skirt on a wide band with 2-inch suspenders, crossed in back and buttoned in front, completes the uniform. Again, bloomer tights may be worn and should be black to match the skirt. Be sure to have the suspenders attached with hooks to the shoulder of the blouse to prevent the straps slipping as you twirl. This uniform costs less than $5.00 for materials.

Gored skirts are attractive. One style I like has contrasting gores (Figure 68). These skirts are even more eye-catching if the gores are inset. The skirt gives a solid-color appearance until a quick turn or small breeze reveals a flash of contrasting color and produces a striking effect.

Sometimes it is advantageous to pattern the uniform after your unit's name. For example, my Diplomats were not sponsored, and most of our appearances were at Japanese festivals or in parades. In order to emphasize the diplomatic

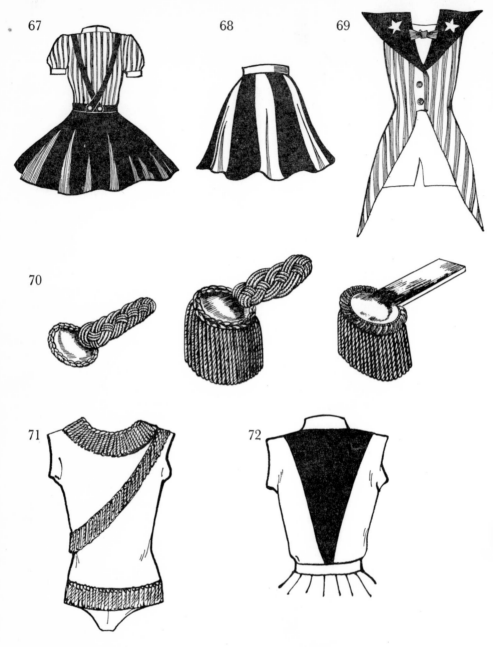

67. Striped blouse and circle skirt.
68. Gored skirt.
69. Cutaway coat and dickey.
70. Epaulettes.
71. Basic leotard decorated with fringe.
72. Blouse decorated with a large V.

mission we were attempting, we designed a brilliant red and white striped cutaway coat with tails to the knees in back (Figure 69). A white dickey was stitched in front with a blue bow tie attached. Blue tight shorts were worn, and the typical "dandy" hat was our headdress. The colors—red, white, and blue—signified our country, the "dandy" hat represented American vaudeville, and the cutaway coat meant "Uncle Sam." This outfit was very colorful and was always well received by our audiences.

If you live in the West, a Western design can be utilized. While there are groups now using Western wear (which means this idea is not original), you can come up with something new and different if you take time with your choices of color and trim.

Shoulder decorations, properly called epaulettes (Figure 70), add zip to your costume. Manufactured epaulettes are expensive but well worth the cost on custom-tailored uniforms. However, something less extravagant is more appropriate for the inexpensive outfits. On a do-it-yourself basis you can have quite handsome epaulettes, but do not expect the finished result to equal the professional ones. A piece of buckram or heavy cardboard is cut out in an epaulette shape. The length of the shoulder must be individually measured. Bright jewel cloth in gold or silver, also cut in an epaulette pattern, is glued onto the buckram or cardboard. Use furniture glue or the instant-drying kind used to make model airplanes. This is an adhesive and does not stain materials. After the glue has dried, stitch gold fringe, about 1″ or 2″ in length, around the outside edge of the epaulette. Do not attach fringe to the shoulder section. Use a strong needle for you will find the glue makes the material very stiff. The finished epaulette is lightly basted across the shoulder seam or attached with a hook and eye. Epaulettes may be added to princess-style dresses as well as to blouses.

Fringe is another item useful in adding glamor to the basic uniform, and it can be used in a number of ways. Decorate the basic leotard, sleeveless and with a round neck, by using contrasting fringe about 2″ long (Figure 71). Stitch it around the neckline and in a pattern from the right shoulder to the waist, and baste three rows around the hips. The imaginative twirler can design unusual and original uniforms by the different placements of fringe.

A large V-shaped piece of shiny jewel cloth, lamé, or plastic patent leather also makes another change for a basic uniform. This is attached at the shoulders with the V point basted at the center of the waist (Figure 72). Cummerbunds or wide belts of the same materials are effective when combined with the V. Much can be done with a lot of imagination and a little money!

Other trims that add elegance to costumes are marabou and bunny fur. They create a luxury look. Although bunny fur is costly, marabou can be purchased for about 75¢ a yard. Braid, frogs, fringe, buckram, jewel cloth, marabou, and practically all supplies can be purchased from theatrical supply houses. If you don't know how to find one in your area, ask a local dance studio. The proprietor should be able to give you all the information you need and might even order your equipment for you.

As you can see from the foregoing there are many styles to choose from. For less expensive uniforms I recommend satin, embossed cotton, or theatrical novelty fabrics. Of course, these materials do not wear or hold their shape as well as standard uniform fabric. If the group is purchasing its own costumes, discussion of costs and styles should be held with the unit. Some groups prefer several inexpensive outfits to one elegant and costly uniform, while others insist that an expensive, finely tailored uniform is necessary to identify the unit.

Although the above are considered indoor uniforms they can be used for outdoor work. The light-weight material and sleeveless tops provide little warmth and in balmy weather they are appropriate. However, when cold winds blow, teeth chatter, goose pimples form, and your arms feel like long icicles when you are trying to spin the baton in winter's wonderland.

Custom-tailored uniforms are smartly cut and perfectly fitted. The heavier gabardines, wools, cashmeres, doeskins,

73. Custom-tailored uniforms.

or combinations of these are always correct and most suitable. A local tailor can be your means of supply, or the school bandmaster can put you in touch with manufacturers specializing in majorette and band outfits. These are naturally expensive because they are perfect in every detail: the jackets are completely lined, the sleeve length is just right, the bodice fits comfortably, skirt lengths are not a fraction of an inch off, and the military collar stands high without binding. Be certain you are completely satisfied with your design and material before ordering. You will be investing your money, and, once the order is placed, it is too late to change your mind.

The fabric of a good custom-tailored uniform holds its press, wears longer, and gives a more professional appearance. You may create your own design and choose your colors from the manufacturer's color chart, or you may select ready-made styles from his catalog. Cost will depend on the materials and accessories you order. The sketches in Figure 73 will give you an idea of the intricate detail that is put into custom-tailored uniforms.

Your uniform, along with your other equipment, must receive loving care which means proper storage (a plastic garment bag, of course) and regular trips to the dry cleaners. Careful pressing at home is a must for a trim appearance. All long-sleeved uniforms should be fitted with shields at the armpits to provide protection to the fabric. You will be so pleased and proud of your uniform that caring for it will be a pleasure.

The most popular type of footwear for the baton performer is the majorette boot. Usually of white elkskin, it has white leather tassels and, on the upper inside of the boot, about 2" of soft felt or fur lining to prevent chafing. The heel is about 1½" high; the sole is sturdy leather. It is extremely well-constructed and designed for long and hard wear. The price varies, depending on the quality of leather and the fur or felt features. For about $12.00 you can buy a boot that will wear for years.

Because the boot is heavy, it will be necessary, after you have perfected your Strut in light practice shoes, to practice

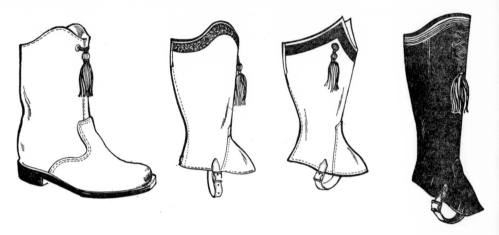

74. Boot-top leggings.

in your boots. By wearing them for practice you become accustomed to the extra weight. When ordering, be sure to specify your shoe size and width or draw an outline on paper of your bare foot. The boot will usually be a full size larger than your regular shoes to allow room for heavy athletic socks. These socks and foot powder are necessary for comfort, for the exertion of marching causes foot perspiration. If blisters develop when you are a novice, soak your feet in warm salt water. This is refreshing, healing, and toughens up tender feet.

White is the most popular color for boots and often is the only color available. If you want to change the color of the tassel to blend with your uniform, this can be easily done. All you need is a heavy piece of cardboard 8″ long and 6″ wide, a ball of yarn or crochet thread, one braided piece of yarn or crochet thread 3″ long, and a single piece 5″ long. Your choice of material depends on the type of tassel you want: yarn makes a heavier-appearing tassel, while crochet makes a less bulky, silkier tassel. To make the tassel, wind the thread around the length of cardboard until it reaches the desired thickness. Don't make it too bulky. Carefully remove the thread from the board and fold in the center, looping the braided piece over the fold. This braided piece goes through the front holes of the boot and ties the tassel in place, hence is braided for extra strength. Measure about $\frac{3}{4}''$ down from the fold and wrap the single strand around the tassel and tie securely. This makes the small ball at the top of the tassel. Clip the loops and even the threads. The tassel is now ready to be fastened securely to the boot. To make multi-colored tassels, merely wind two or three different-colored threads together at the same time.

Some marching groups use boot-top leggings (Figure 74). The styles of these vary. They fit snugly over an ordinary shoe, and are made to order. They are usually of calfskin with a zipper back closing, and have a contrasting top trim and tassel. Prices vary, depending on quality of leather, style, and height. I have made boot-top leggings out of heavy oilcloth to match uniform colors, and also from heavy buckram with uniform material glued or stitched to the buckram. These are adequate for stage work, but they are not durable or strong enough for parades.

To make your own leggings, cut a pattern with two side pieces and one center piece. The size of the pattern is determined by your calf, ankle, and the length you want. The pattern should be about $4''$ larger than the exact measurement to allow for seams, zipper, and a roomy legging. The two side pieces are stitched down the center front; the center piece, which is cut in a half circle at the front of the foot, is stitched into place; and the jacket-type zipper is placed in the back. A piece of elastic is sewed to each side under the arch to hold the legging in place. These do not, of course, have the professional detail of the custom-made designs, but they do provide an inexpensive change in your appearance for stage work. If your group orders boot-top leggings, specify the ankle and calf measurements, shoe size, and the length you desire. Don't forget to indicate the color for trim and tassel. These leggings may be ordered in black or white. Your teacher, bandmaster, or local music store can doubtless put you in touch with a supplier, and the appendix of this book lists names and addresses of others.

Proper care of boots or leggings is important for that smart appearance. Leggings fold easily, and can be stored in plastic bags. Be sure they are clean when put away. Keep your boots a sparkling white and take time with your polish application. A sloppy job is always noticeable. Don't neglect the brown leather side soles and heels when polishing. Your boot completes your appearance, and even the most expensive uniform seems shabby if boots are not given proper care. When not in use, store your boots in a plastic bag, and keep crumpled tissue or newspaper in the foot part to hold its shape. Your boots are important to you, so do take good care of them.

Opinions differ on the wearing of head coverings. I feel that a uniform is not complete without a headdress. Others hold that a hat of any kind is a nuisance—it can fall off or slip to an unbecoming angle and thus be an additional worry to the wearer. However, if a hat is the proper size and secured firmly, it will not fall off or slip, and, once you are accustomed to it, you will have no trouble. The decision on wearing head coverings is, of course, up to the group.

You may choose from a wide range of styles from the high shako to the small overseas cap. A shako (Figure 75) is a tall hat, covered in white polar bear cloth, sparkle plastic, or shako fabric, with a brim and usually some type of emblem fastened in the center front and a saucy plume on the top. It has adjustable chin straps, a suction-type sweat band, and usually an adjustable head-sizing device. There are many kinds of shakos, plumes, and emblems for your consideration. Cost depends on material and the type of plume and emblem. If shakos are purchased, a large storage box is necessary and may be ordered along with the hat, or you may secure a covered box from a local department store.

Returning to the limited budget theme, shako frames, made of heavy buckram, can be purchased and are simple to cover. Cut the material in three pieces: the top, the brim, and the body of the shako. Use quick-drying glue to fasten the material to the frame. Add a gay plume on top, an emblem in front if you wish, and you have an inexpensive shako. The variety of plumes at theatrical supply houses is not as wide as at the uniform manufacturers.

The extremely tall hat worn by drum majorettes and drum majors is the busby (Figure 75). Covered with white fur,

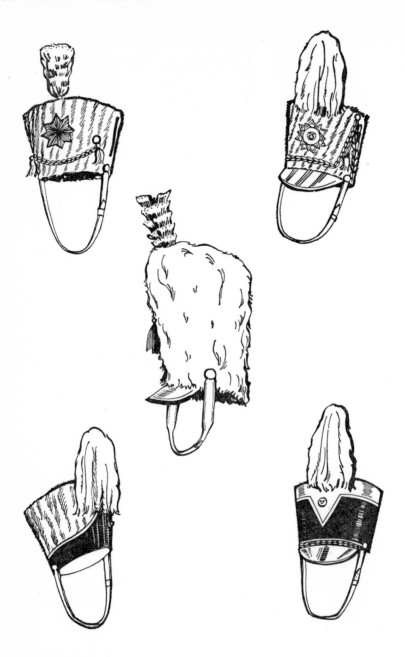

75. Shakos and a busby (center).

76

77

78

76. Pillbox.   77. Overseas caps.   78. Tams.

this hat is really beautiful and, although over 14″ tall, is surprisingly light in weight. Most busbies are designed on a cane frame. If you decide on a busby, remember that all acrobatic work and much leg work will be eliminated from routines because its height interferes with certain twirling executions. You are limited to basics, Stationaries, and Signals. Don't attempt any trick work.

The pillbox (Figure 76), sometimes called a topper, is a favorite kind of headwear. This hat is about 3″ or 4″ high, and fits snugly around the head. It is usually worn tilted to the right or left. Like the shako, it is very stiff, and it is covered with the same material as the uniform. Frames can be purchased and covered very simply. In desperation, I have used oatmeal boxes to make pillboxes by cutting 3″ from the bottom of the boxes. When the material was glued on, only the wearer knew that under that pert topper was part of a rolled oats cookie recipe. A small plastic bag makes a perfect storage container.

There are many kinds of caps (Figure 77): the overseas, Belgian overseas, pointed overseas, and the WAC type, all similar in appearance. When custom-tailored, they are made of the same material as the uniforms but without stiff frames. They are easy to wear because of their light weight and are favored by units that specialize in jumps and acrobatics. They fold into a small parcel for storing.

If you wish to make your own pillboxes or overseas caps, buckram for the frames can be purchased from theatrical suppliers, and the material glued on. Hats made this way will be stiff.

Berets and tams (Figures 78) are becoming and unusual. The French tam and the tam with a visor are two types occasionally used by marching units. The French tam usually sits off the forehead but can be worn at a saucy angle. The visor tam is, of course, worn straight.

There are numerous kinds of emblems that may be purchased for headwear (Figure 79). On tall shakos, a large gold or silver emblem is striking. For other hats, smaller emblems such as harps, eagles, buttons, or crests are more appropriate.

79

80

79. Emblems for headgear.   80. Shoulder decorations.

81

82

83

81. Pleated shoulder sash.   82. Cape.   83. Whistle on a chain.

Full length capes (Figure 82) are practical and serve several purposes. They keep you warm as toast while you are waiting for an outdoor performance, they protect the uniform from dust, and they keep the design and style of your uniform as a surprise for the audience. Capes are usually knee length, have high military collars, are cut full, and are lined in contrasting materials. They can be custom-tailored or made at home, and should match the uniform. These capes are never worn while performing, but they are so welcome after a half-time football performance on a frosty winter day.

Shoulder decorations give a dash to plain uniforms. A pleated shoulder sash (Figure 81), or the always popular epaulette, or trefoil shoulder knots are yours for the choosing (Figure 80).

A rain cape is a most practical accessory. These transparent plastic capes are cut very full and are hooded to protect the uniform, headgear, and the wearer from disagreeable weather.

A whistle is, of course, a necessity for leaders and drum majorettes, and is attached to a good-looking chain or ribbon matched to the uniform (Figure 83).

There is so much variety offered in uniforms and accessories. Use good taste and common sense in your selections, and your group will look sharp!

Your name, initials, or some type of identification should be placed on every piece of your clothing. It is a good idea to include the group's name and address in case equipment is misplaced at a competition or convention. On uniforms this mark can be placed just below the collar band of the blouse and also just below the waist band of the skirt and shorts.

Now that you have assembled a complete uniform, remember that it represents a lot of time, thought, work, and money. Give it good care and wear it with pride.

13

Competitions and Conventions

COMPETITIONS are wonderful in every way. They are exciting, fun, and educational. Here you are judged by experts who give both helpful criticism and praise. Here you have an opportunity to meet students from other areas, and the knowledge you gain in this exchange of ideas, twirls, and routines is priceless.

If you request, your grading sheet is given to you. A study of this will help you to correct any irregularities the judges noted in your performance.

Although competitions are usually organized by baton schools, you do not have to be a member of the school to enter. Neither do you have to be an advanced or outstanding twirler. Competing units are divided by age and experience into categories from beginners to advanced students. The number of years or months you have twirled is the basis on which you are placed in the proper level. All participants have equal chances. Persons associated in any way with baton schools never sit as judges. A point system of judging is used and is completely fair and without favoritism.

Winners and second and third place twirlers are awarded handsome trophies, usually bronze statues or pins in various designs. You are judged on a number of things: technique, originality, appearance, style, strutting, speed, and presentation. If you have practiced your competition routine to the point of polished perfection, this, plus your confidence, will get you through with flying colors.

Competitions are held annually, usually in the early spring. In the appendix you will find listed some of the organizations which will be happy to place you on their mailing lists or send you information regarding competitions.

A typical invitation to a competition might include the following:

1) Name and address of the school where the competition will be held.

2) Names of the contest hosts.

3) Names and addresses of the judges (usually selected from many different areas).

4) Competition agenda including dates and times: (a) briefing of judges is first on the list and includes an explanation of the point system used and a question period; (b) competition time schedule; (c) trophy awards.

5) Entrance fees and spectator charges. To finance competitions, a fee is charged for each event entered, and spectators pay admission. No profits are made, and even judges donate their time.

6) Groupings (sample listing):

BATON SOLO: Entrance fee $1.50. Time limit $2\frac{1}{2}$ minutes. (You must keep your routine within the time limits. It can not run too short or too long. A competition is organized on a specific timetable, and each twirler must adhere to that schedule. If you do not keep within the limit specified, you are marked down by the judges.)

Age Divisions	*Experience and Training Division*
Pee Wee (pre-school)	Beginners: those who have not twirled over six months.
Novice (age 6, 7, 8)	Semi-intermediate: those who have twirled not over 1 1/2 years and have never won any place in a contest.
Juvenile (age 9, 10, 11)	Same as above
Junior (age 12, 13, 14)	Same as above
Senior (age 15 and over)	Intermediate: those who have won in a beginner contest.

Semi-advanced: those who have won in an intermediate contest.

Advanced: those who have won in any major contest.

Senior beginner (age 15 and over) — Those who twirled for not over a period of 1 1/2 years and have never placed or won a contest.

(As you see, the units are broken down by age and experience, and there is a place for each twirler.)

BOYS (Two divisions to be decided upon later): Although baton twirling is for boys and girls both, its popularity seems much greater with the feminine gender. There are often not enough boys so it is impossible to list the divisions until all entries are received. At that time, the contest hosts will break down the boys' division by age and experience.

TWO BATONS: Entrance fee $1.50. Time limit 1½ minutes.

Age Division	*Experience and Training Division*
Novice and juvenile combined, 11 and under	Beginners never having entered or placed higher than third.
Junior and senior combined, 12 and over	Advanced.

This is obviously for advanced students since it goes without saying that anyone capable of handling two batons skillfully has studied for some time or has spent countless hours practicing. A shorter time limit is set for this routine because 1½ minutes with two batons is quite enough time to exhibit your skill.

PAIRS: Entrance fee $2.50 per pair. Time limit 2½ minutes.

Age Division	*Experience and Training Division*
Novice and juveniles combined, 11 and under	Beginners who have twirled not over 1 1/2 years.

Junior and senior combined, Advanced.
12 and over

TEAMS: Entrance fee $1.25 per person. Time limit $2\frac{1}{2}$ minutes (three to five persons).

Age Division	*Experience and Training Division*
Novice and juvenile combined, 11 and under	Beginners who have twirled not over 1 1/2 years.
Junior and senior combined, 12 and over	Advanced.

Here is where precision really counts. If you do simple twirls with precision, you give a much better performance than if you do difficult ones in a ragged manner.

STRUT: Entrance fee $1.50. Time limit 1 minute.

Age Division

Novice and juvenile combined, 11 and under
Junior and senior combined, 12 and over
You are judged on how you step out: your body stance, your "style." Corners must be squared off, and you must stay with your beat.

BATON NOVELTY: Entrance fee $1.50. Time limit 2 minutes. Anything you can do with a standard baton that is novel is acceptable: tap dancing, acrobatics, etc. No flags, hoops, or fire batons permitted.

Age Division

Novice and juvenile combined, 11 and under
Junior and senior combined, 12 and over
Originality and technique are the bases of judgment in this event.

NOVELTY BATON: Entrance fee $1.50. Time limit $2\frac{1}{2}$ minutes. Different types of batons, such as hoop, ribbon, etc., are used in this contest. In some areas the fire baton is permitted. This depends entirely on local rules and regulations that govern the contest hosts.
2 divisions: 11 and under, 12 and over

SHOW ROUTINES: Entrance fee $1.00 a person. Time limit 5 minutes (corps of five or more).

Age Division

Novice and juvenile combined, 11 and under
Junior and senior combined, 12 and over
This is usually a stage routine set to music other than a march. You are judged on your general appearance and precision rather than on twirling ability.

FLAG SWINGING: Entrance fee $1.50. Time limit $2\frac{1}{2}$ minutes.
Age Divisions if there are enough entries.
Swiss or baton flag swinging may be used.

You may enter as many divisions for which you are qualified as you wish. When all entrants have completed their performances, score cards are tallied for the trophy presentations—the highlight of the evening. Not everyone can win, but each entrant has gained in knowledge and experience. If you are a lucky winner, don't forget to give a snappy Salute as you accept your award. Most competitions are covered by the local press, and the write-ups and pictures are good material for your scrapbook.

The reverse side of the invitation is usually an entry blank. It is worded in this manner:

Name	Age	
Address	City	State
Teacher, if any		
Years of experience		

Solo beginner (   ) Semi-intermediate (   ) Semi-advanced (   ) Advanced (   )
Boys (   ) Two Batons (   ) Beginner (   ) Advanced (   )
Pairs: Beginner (   ) Advanced (   )
Groups: Beginner (   ) Advanced (   ) Groups of five or more (   ) Strut (   ) Baton Novelty Solo (   )
Novelty Baton (   )
Show Routines (   ) Baton Novelty group (   )
Flag (   )

Indicate the divisions you and your group are entering and mail the entry form and fees to the hosts of the competition. There is usually a date limit on entries because the organizers must have time to assign each entrant to the proper category. In competitions there are no on-the-spot entries because of the need for previous planning.

This should give you some idea of competition organization. I urge you to enter competitions, not only because winning is a rewarding and thrilling experience but because the ideas you get in competing improve your twirling ability and add to your knowledge. You can also organize your own competitions! Follow the above format, send out invitations, buy the trophies, select the judges, and *remember* to plan it well in advance.

CONVENTIONS

Conventions are most often held in the summer months. These are sometimes sponsored by large baton schools or by baton organizations. They are attended by teachers as well as students, and usually last for a week or two. They might be called baton clinics: ideas are exchanged, new twirls taught, different techniques and styles presented in both twirling and marching, and often many little faults you are unaware of are corrected. Conventions are regional so you should have no trouble finding one not too far from your home. Every day you are attending a convention you are learning something new. It is smart to have your baton notebook on hand to make notes of new twirls and variations. You will not be able to perfect each new idea during the convention because you will want to collect as much information as possible. After you have returned home, you can practice these new tricks. The very top baton experts are on hand to demonstrate the latest developments. The time spent at a convention can provide enough new material to last for many months.

There is, of course, an entry fee for conventions. This is necessary to defray the expenses of space rental and printed material. At most conventions, the experts are volunteers who donate their experience and time. Entry fees vary in different localities. Check the appendix in this book for convention information in your area.

Sometimes a group will send only one member to the convention or competition. She relays all the knowledge she has acquired to the entire unit when she comes back. A teacher often chooses one or two advanced students to accompany her to a convention, thus enabling the school to be represented in all scheduled events. Occasionally a sponsor will send the whole group.

Competition invitations and convention notices are mailed to all baton schools, organizations, and interested individuals. Write the appropriate organization nearest to you and have your group's name put on their mailing list. You will receive a great deal of helpful information to keep you advised and abreast of the times in the baton twirling world.

14

Showmanship and Sportsmanship

IN A DISCUSSION on the requirements of a baton twirler we must certainly mention showmanship and sportsmanship.

What is showmanship? The late Al Jolson defined it as "likeability," and this is a wonderful definition. Many times you've watched an actually mediocre entertainer with the feeling that he was the greatest. He is projecting so much personality and "likeability" to the audience that all he really needs to do is walk on stage and smile.

Showmanship must be learned. Some people have a natural knack for projecting their personalities, while others must spend time practicing until they are confident or at ease enough to reach from the stage to the hearts of the audience.

The cleverest baton twirler sometimes will be received with less enthusiasm than a beginner because the latter's personality is more pleasing. A winning smile is a must. This does not mean a forced "cheese" expression. The smile must come from the heart. When you are thoroughly enjoying what you are doing, the audience knows it and shares your obvious pleasure. A relaxed attitude produces a relaxed audience, and tension is equally contagious. Outward poise and calmness are the trademarks of the experienced performer even though butterflies are fluttering in her tummy.

Your first public appearance may be a nightmare for you. Little worries creep around in your mind, and your palms on which you depend for good twirling are wet with perspiration. You imagine your baton flying across the auditorium into the crowd, drops landing in the orchestra pit, perhaps even boots or hats falling off. Usually, none of this ever happens. Although you may not feel the least bit relaxed in your first appearance, you will find that once you have started your routine, you can smile and you are able to make a graceful bow. Confidence comes with repeated performances, and soon *you* will be projecting a winning personality and warm atmosphere to the coldest of crowds.

There is really such a thing as a cold audience. It seems restless, bored, unattentive, perhaps even noisy. This is sensed immediately by the performer. Under these circumstances, a baton twirler might develop a "care less" attitude and give a poor performance. This must *not* happen. In fact you must put forth more effort and do your utmost to win the audience. And when you do this, you feel the coolness start to melt and a warm responsiveness take its place. *Your* showmanship has won the hearts of the crowd.

When you have reached the point where your twirling is done without the need for concentration, your body stance is automatic, and your movements smooth and coordinated, it is time to start practicing in front of a mirror. You may notice that you are making odd facial expressions or frowning or moving your body too much. Your mirror tells all, and you can see how you appear to others. Correct your bad habits! Use the mirror too to develop your Poses. You will soon see which is your best arm angle, your best approach to a difficult leg trick, and that even a slight tilt of the head makes a different appearance. Keep in mind that the mirror is a means of perfecting your style, but it does not take the place of an audience. Projecting personality, which brings forth your "likeability," can only be done in front of a live crowd!

Showmanship means too that in your performance there will be no pauses, no monotonous repetitions. The pace will be so snappy that the viewers will watch attentively. If there are several baton groups on the program, each unit must be original and different. Remember, you can always learn by watching other units. Never feel that your group has reached such a point of superiority that others are not worth studying.

Just as being too shy is a handicap to a group's acceptance, so, too, is being too arrogant. A unit that appears conscious of its importance onstage is quickly rejected. You must have confidence in your ability to project and entertain, but you must never exhibit self-satisfaction or smugness. Regardless of how outstanding your performance is, you should show humility to your teammates and the spectators. A radiant smile, a gracious way, a poised and calm manner, style in performance, originality in delivery, and a grateful attitude will develop showmanship, that "likeability" so important to a performer.

Although baton twirling is an art and a skill and not a sport, a great amount of sportsmanship is necessary in your work. In group work you are a team, working with teammates, and consideration for other performers is a must. Your attitude is reflected throughout the entire group. If another girl is given the solo you feel is really yours, it does no good to sulk about it. Continue your good twirling and the time will come when you too are recognized. Patience, too, is important in team work. If some members of the unit are having difficulty in executing a twirl, it is necessary for the entire group to repeat and repeat the twirl to develop uniform precision. If you take the attitude "Well, I can do it, why should I keep practicing it?" you are showing poor sportsmanship. Remember, the next time it might be you who needs repetition and practice to master a certain twirl. When drops occur during a performance, glares at the unlucky offender have no audience appeal whatever. The dropper should recover her baton as quickly as possible, perhaps making a nice little bow, while the group continues with the routine. "A dancer is never considered a pro until she has fallen down onstage." This also applies to twirlers and baton drops.

Most units find it satisfying to create their own routines. They know their own special skills, recognize where they excel, and can thus arrange various twirls into a suitable sequence for a better performance. Many teachers let their units design their routines, offering suggestions on style or presenting ideas only when the group seems to be at a loss.

Again, sportsmanship is involved for it is natural for each to have her favorite trick, Pose, or twirl and be inclined to include it. Acceptance of what is best for the group and responsiveness to others' wishes are essential.

When you are a solo performer, it is especially important that you exhibit good sportsmanship. You may not have the spot on the program you want, or perhaps someone else is using the same music you selected, or wearing a uniform identical with yours. All this must be taken in stride with no display of temper, resentment, or disappointment.

Before a performance or contest, when everyone is a little nervous and edgy, there is usually an air of tenseness backstage. It is easy in this atmosphere for tempers to flare. My Jet-ettes developed a most unique way to overcome these pre-performance jitters. Our performances were usually given before an all-Japanese audience and, along with our normal worries, we never knew exactly when we were scheduled to appear because of the language barrier. Interpretation was not always clear or was misunderstood. Many times our music cue would come in the opening of the show when we were sure that we were the fourth or last number on the program. One of our members suggested that the moments before show time be called "Praise Time," and during this wait members would compliment each other on particular bits of twirling observed during recent practices and classes. This was our only "Praise Time," and the effect was wonderful. Every girl beamed as she marched onto the stage, feeling confident of herself and a warm sense of companionship toward the other members.

Praise is wonderful, but it must be sincere. Compliments on work that does not come up to one's usual standard do as much harm as carping criticism. When a group has put much effort into mastering a twirl, compliments are due when it is perfected, but not until then.

The qualities we listed away back in the beginning of this book—interest, enthusiasm, patience, and consideration of others—all add up, as you can see, to good sportsmanship.

THE CLOSING PITCH

Now that you have studied this book which is the result of my many years of study, training, and performing, you realize that you *can* organize a twirling unit even if a qualified teacher is not available. It will be more difficult, of course, because you will not have professional advice and experience to fall back on. Your progress may not be as rapid and you may have to extend your course to a longer period, but a do-it-yourself baton group is a goal you can readily achieve. Your leadership, the group's keen interest and enthusiasm, and this book to guide you will produce a precision unit of which you may be justly proud.

Remember, as self-taught students, you must do more than merely teach. You just be able to look objectively at what you accomplish and must never be satisfied with any phase of the work until you are masters of it. You must never be content with average proficiency when you know you have the capability to excel. You have discovered that baton twirling is not learned in a short space of time. Like any other art or skill, it must be studied, developed, and perfected. Like any other subject, it must be understood, and, like any other phase of exhibition work, it must be practiced. And, because you are self-taught, you will have a greater feeling of achievement because your success is due entirely to your own efforts.

Months later, as the drum rolls and the performance starts, you will step out with pride. You have mastered an art and acquired a skill. Display your achievements with confidence as you spin the silver shaft!

15

Suggestions to Teachers, Organizers, and Leaders

A GOOD teacher has been defined as one who makes himself progressively unnecessary. How true this statement is when applied to baton twirling.

As students progress and reach an advanced stage of twirling, teachers bow out of the picture. Whether working in a large baton school or teaching a group of neighborhood children in the garage, all of us are striving for the same purpose: to develop and train a baton student to the point of perfection and proficiency. It is a challenging job and a most rewarding one. In my opinion, anyone who works with children is a fortunate being. The children's sincere appreciation, their frank opinions, and their heart-warming response make teaching them a joy. Our work is not easy: we must have an unusual amount of patience, we must keep our explanations at the students' level, and we must have the ability to break down complicated twirls so that they are readily grasped by the pupil. We must also have a real understanding of both children and parents and be able to get on with both equally well. Above all, we must have high standards, so that along with baton training we contribute to the development of our students' characters.

Novice teachers usually start their careers with their heads full of theory and application of theory. Experience soon proves that theory is fine but does not always apply.

Only through experience do we gain in teaching knowledge and only through experience do we find our own best methods of presentation, explanation, and class management.

Each teacher has a different system. What is right for one is not always suitable for another. Regardless of the methods used, each instructor must be explicit in her explanations, must demonstrate slowly, and must keep the entire approach at the students' level. One might be an exceptionally good twirler and not a good teacher. It is an art to take your thoughts completely out of yourself and project them to your students.

I have yet to meet a teacher, whether she is a beginner or one who has been instructing for years, from whom I have not gained some type of knowledge. Different ways of presentation or of handling classes, or of arranging programs or routines can be learned through conversations or visits with other teachers.

I have developed a class format which I shall pass along to you. Through my many years of teaching I find this schedule works best for me. Perhaps you may choose to follow it or adapt it in some ways to meet your needs. However, you may have such a successful format of your own that you have no reason to change.

My classes are scheduled for one hour: 45 minutes for instruction and 15 minutes for questions and/or individual help. I insist that students report to class ready to work. We do not waste any time during our class period. We are assembled to learn baton twirling, and everything else is secondary.

Although there is a warm friendliness in the classroom, firmness prevails. There is no gum chewing, candy eating, or soda-pop drinking. Each student has been previously assigned her place in the room, and, when the door opens, the children waiting outside know it is time for their class and they assemble quickly in their proper places. Roll is called, and we proceed with our beginning exercises.

I am very stuffy about tardiness and, from the very first lesson, I stress punctuality. This is for the pupils' benefit, not mine. When a student wanders in late, she disrupts the entire class, and it takes several minutes to brief the tardy person on what we have already done and what we are working on now. Just prior to our 15-minute question and individual help period, we end our class with a Baton Salute. This is our way of thanking each other for a nice lesson. After the Salute, those who have not been asked to stay for extra help and those who have no questions are dismissed, and they leave promptly. The rest work for the additional time. Then the door is opened so that the next group knows it is time for its lesson. You cannot permit students from preceding or following classes to roam around the classroom. It is not fair to the group you are instructing. It is important to keep classes on schedule. Most people are busy, and parents who have to pick up a child at a certain time do not appreciate having to wait 15 or 20 minutes because a class was started late or is running overtime.

A syllabus of instruction helps you keep classes within a 45-minute period. Of course, groups do vary and some can speed through twirls which others take a longer time to learn. However, you can usually keep close to your schedule. I set mine on a ten-week period. Before starting my classes, I have prepared a ten-week guide, indicating exactly what I expect each class to accomplish during the course. Often I have overestimated, and we do not complete all the planned twirls. Other times I have underestimated my students' dedicated progress, and we complete the first ten-week syllabus in a shorter period and go into the next course. With such a guide, classes stay organized, for you are never in a quandary as to which phase of twirling to present next. Lessons take much advance planning. You cannot just go to class and teach. A great deal of thought must be given to what should be presented to each class and when it should be presented. In my early days as a teacher, I found I expected entirely too much from my students. Time, age, and experience have taught me to be more patient, more understanding, and less demanding. Time, age, and experience have also taught me how to be firm and yet kind.

It is necessary to maintain good parent-teacher relationships. When you are working with another person's child, you are working with her most precious possession. Feelings can easily be hurt when children are involved, and misunderstandings result. Always take time to answer phone calls or notes from parents. They are naturally interested in their children's progress, and, although you might feel your knowledge or ability is being questioned, this is not usually the case. Once the problem is discussed frankly, you will find that parents are more than willing to accept your advice and reasoning. If such discussion is delayed or avoided, ill-will could develop.

Each teacher has her own opinion on parents watching class instruction. I allow parents to observe whenever they wish to, but I tell them beforehand that there must be no talking or other distractions. I have learned that some students excel when their parents are watching, while others seem to "freeze" and give an inferior performance. I have also learned that as the child progresses, parents discontinue classroom visits, preferring to observe achievements at the end of the term program.

Programs are important to the student. Even though they are only small get-togethers at the school with parents as the audience, they mean much to the progress of the twirler. Not only does she get a special thrill out of appearing in front of a crowd, but she is also acquiring stage presence and showmanship. I usually plan one small program during the Christmas holidays, limited to parents and students. After the program, ice cream and cookies, cokes and coffee are served. Here parents may meet and talk with me in a relaxed atmosphere. It is at this time we usually exchange our class Christmas gifts, and have Santa Claus on hand to add to the festivities. Our principal program is held in May or June at the completion of the term, and at this time we invite the general public. In this program every student participates, uniformed smartly, and we try to present the show on a most professional level. This is the reward for all the hard work throughout the term. Certificates of achievement are presented to qualifying students. Of course, our advanced groups perform frequently during the year at numerous public functions, and they add their talents to these programs.

Summer months, which are usually crowded months for both teachers and students, do not permit much baton activity. I like to attend conventions whenever possible, meet with other teachers, take a well-earned rest, and prepare for the next term. Students, however, cannot spend the entire summer without practice. For this reason I hold a Baton Clinic for two three-week periods during the summer, one after the Fourth of July holiday and the other at the end of August. At Baton Clinic we do not progress into new work. We strive to develop better techniques and styles in the twirls we have already learned. A baton clinic is to the student what a convention is to a teacher.

When teaching you are apt to forget about yourself and suddenly you find that your own speed has decreased considerably, for you seldom do any twirl fast while demonstrating. You also develop little faults and bad habits that you are not aware of. A few weeks at a convention, working with other teachers, will bring these things to light, and you will be able to correct them before they become a set pattern. Attending a convention can be so inspiring that you return home eager for the next term to start. You have a wealth of new information and ideas which you are anxious to share!

I am a firm believer in the use of tape recorders for teaching, while many of my colleagues prefer record players. The advantage of the tape recorder is advance preparation. By referring to the syllabus and using tape, I am able to prepare each class's music ahead of time. Individual tapes are made for each group, and often I tape ten weeks of lessons in advance.

A teacher may invest in various methods of advertising: newpaper, radio, or television, but the best means is a satisfied parent telling an interested parent of the teacher's skills and abilities. Creating goodwill in the community is also important. This can be done in several ways. For example, you could help a local high school organize a twirling group, plan their routines, and assist with their practices even if the girls are not your students. Courtesies that you extend are always returned in some way, you will learn. Never be too busy to answer questions about twirling. If your advice is sought, be kind enough to give all the information you possibly can, even if the questions come from another teacher, an organizer, or perhaps someone planning to start rival classes. There is room for all, and competition keeps us on our toes.

Your own marching group is another excellent means of calling attention to your baton school. Once a class has advanced to the point where you can form a unit, do so. Uniform it smartly and give it a very showy routine. Every public performance will add more students to your enrollment.

In school management, costs and expenses must be watched closely. Overhead can eat into your income to the point that your joy in teaching is offset by "please remit" notices. A teacher must be a good manager and bookkeeper. Expensive quarters with elegant furnishings are not necessary. It is what the student learns within the walls that counts. A convenient location is, of course, desirable. Many cities and towns have public halls that may be rented for a small fee.

Until a teacher is well established, she should never count on class fees until they are paid. Later, an established teacher may know almost to the penny what her enrollment will bring in. Experience has taught her what percentage of former students will return, how many new students will enroll, and how many drop-outs there will be. It is not unusual to start with a very small enrollment, so the novice teacher should not be discouraged. Her skill and ability will soon be mentioned by one child to another, by one parent to another, and her enrollment will grow steadily and rapidly.

Remember also to keep down costs to the parents. Plan program uniforms economically, and have them designed in such a way that they can be worn for several performances. My students buy their equipment a bit at a time. For example, the beginner needs a baton and practice clothes when she starts her first lesson, but majorette boots can be acquired at a later date. My classes recognize added equipment more or less as a reward for progress, and the initial outlay of cash is not too hard on the parents.

Always keep your students interested and enthusiastic—never let them get bored. I believe when classes start lagging, it is the teacher's fault, not the students'. The instructor should quickly reappraise her methods and attitude and take action. There are many things you can do when you sense that interest is dropping. Invite in a guest teacher —this often gives the group a lift—or organize a competition, even if it is limited to your own students.

A successful teacher does not think of her students only at class time. A small card file can keep information on birthdays, and a little card mailed to the pupil is a thoughtful gesture which is always appreciated. When illness strikes, and a child misses several lessons, often it is impossible for the teacher to visit the sick room. It takes just a few minutes to write a note or select an appropriate card to let the student know she is remembered and missed.

A leader—that is a member of the group who has been chosen by the unit to that position—works very closely with the teacher, and often it is the leader who carries out the teacher's instructions at practice. A good leader respects and follows her teacher's advice. If a group has no teacher, it is the leader who must accept the teacher's responsibilities concerning schedules, practice, routines, etc. However, the leader must remember that she only leads the group; she does not dictate to it. She is always ready to follow the group's suggestions and carry through the leading and signaling when routines have been set to the unit's approval. The leader should never adopt the attitude of "I'm leader, I'm boss." This is a good way to get voted out of leadership.

An organizer—one who has had no baton training, but has a desire to form a twirling group—has even more responsibilities. In addition to organizing the unit, she must accept the duties of the teacher. She sets the practice times, trains the group, makes all the decisions. By following the format teachers use as set forth above, she can produce a unit she will be proud of, but she must realize that much effort, time, and a dedicated spirit are needed. She must remember to give instructions clearly and to be sure they are understood by every pupil. She must demonstrate slowly so that every movement of the wrist, foot, arm, or body is comprehended. I often use student-demonstrators in very large classes, and an organizer may also do this, utilizing an advanced student to teach a beginner. A student-demonstrator gains from this arrangement as does the teacher.

Teaching baton twirling requires a lot of planning and hard work, but watching your pupils' progress is rewarding and working with children keeps you young at heart.

Appendix

FURTHER information regarding schools, teachers, conventions, and competitions in your area, as well as details on uniforms and equipment, may be obained by writing to the parties listed below:

Altus School of Dance
Betty Turner, Director
1105 Asa Lee
Altus, Okla.

Bon Mar Supplies
519 Stone St.
Walla Walla, Wash.

Drum Major Magazine
Minneapolis, Minn.

Kent Schools
Bonnie Kent, Director
206 E. Main
Walla Walla, Wash.

Kraskin Baton Co.
753 Lyndale Ave.
South Minneapolis, Minn.

Ludwig and Co.
1728 No. Damen Ave.
Chicago 47, Ill.

National Association of Dance
   and Affiliated Arts
1920 West 3rd
Los Angeles, Calif.

National Baton Twirlers Association
Don Sartell, Director
Jonesville, Wisc.

Ostwald Inc.
Ostwald Building
Staten Island 1
New York, N.Y.

Southern Exporters and Importers
1809 Louisiana St.
Houston, Tex.

Style Queen Inc.
Att: Douglas Armitage
1536 Seventh St.
Los Angeles 17, Calif.

United States Twirlers Assoc.
Att: Trudy Smith
Sharpsville, Ind.

Wolff and Fording Theatrical Supplies
46 Stuart St.
Boston, Mass.

Index